Implementing restorative justice in children's residential care

Carol Hayden and Dennis Gough

First published in Great Britain in 2010 by The Policy Press

The Policy Press
University of Bristol
Fourth Floor, Beacon House
Queen's Road
Bristol BS8 1QU
UK

t: +44 (0)117 331 4054
f: +44 (0)117 331 4093
tpp-info@bristol.ac.uk
www.policypress.co.uk

North American office:
The Policy Press
c/o International Specialized Books Services
920 NE 58th Avenue, Suite 300
Portland, OR 97213-3786, USA
t: +1 503 287 3093, f: +1 503 280 8832
info@isbs.com

© The Policy Press 2010

ISBN 978 1 84742 648 2

British Library Cataloguing in Publication Data
A catalogue record for this report is available from the British Library.

Library of Congress Cataloging-in-Publication Data
A catalog record for this report has been requested.

The right of Carol Hayden and Dennis Gough to be identified as authors of this
work has been asserted by them in accordance with Sections 77 and 78 of the
1988 Copyright, Designs and Patents Act.

Cover image courtesy of iStockphoto®
Cover design by Qube Design Associates, Bristol
Printed in Great Britain by Hobbs, Southampton

1/5/11

Contents

List of figures and tables

Figures

Tables

Acknowledgements

Many people helped set up contacts and collect the data in this research, although most of them cannot be named because it was agreed not to identify the location of the study. One exception is Rachel Forrester, who worked as a research assistant during the second period of the fieldwork. The authors would like to thank her and everyone else whose work helped them acquire the range and depth of data reported in this study. Thanks also to the local authority and care home managers who allowed the authors access to the care homes where the research was carried out.

Restorative justice: promises and pathways

Introduction

This chapter reviews some of the main themes within the vast literature on restorative justice (RJ). It charts the rise of the concept and the main areas where RJ is seen as a more satisfactory way to respond to harmful and criminal behaviour than the conventional criminal justice system. The chapter notes the various guises that the paradigm has taken to date. It focuses on key values, processes and outcomes required for a thorough understanding of how to conceptualise RJ. It highlights some of the key evidence about impact and outcomes, noting an increased emphasis on reducing recidivism in policy formulations of the approach, as well as reviews of the available research. The chapter goes on to look at the place of RJ within contemporary youth justice systems. Finally, the specific application of RJ and context of the current research – children's residential care – is considered.

The rise and promise of restorative justice

Restorative justice has developed into one of the most exciting and hopeful ways of responding to law breaking and harmful behaviour in recent decades. The appeal and growth of RJ approaches and schemes has been so pronounced as to be described as no less than a 'global social movement' and a 'restorative justice boom' (Robinson and Shapland, 2008, p 337). RJ has advanced from being a powerful critique of the professionalised criminal justice system and has extended its reach into repairing state conflict and harmonising civil society. RJ is seen as a transformative approach to mending the harm and rupture in post-conflict societies such as the post-Apartheid South Africa and post-war Balkan states. It is also increasingly valued as an equally transformative approach to conflicts in school, family life and the community and, in our research, child welfare and state care. Indeed, as we document here, restorative justice has been seen to be a key 'solution' to the much-needed transformation of the 'state parent'. Given this range of applications, RJ could be said to be in danger of becoming 'aerosol' words, sprayed over difficult and often intractable social problems by policy makers convinced of its 'Nirvana-like' transformative potential in a diverse range of environments to eliminate problems and make things better (Daly, 2002). The dizzying variety of environments, problems and conflict in which RJ has been used and its subsequent adaptations is best encapsulated by Daly and Immarigeon (1998):

> Over the last two decades, 'restorative justice' has emerged in varied guises with different names, and in many countries; it has sprung from sites of activism, academia, and justice system workplaces. The concept may refer to analternative process of resolving disputes, to alternative sanctioning options, or to a distinctly different, new model of criminal justice organised around principles of restoration to victims, offenders and the communities in which they live. It may refer to diversion from formal court processes, to actions taken in parallel with court decisions, and to meetings between offenders and victims at any stage of the criminal process. (p 21)

What is also interesting is that the rise in interest in RJ, both in the academic community and among policy makers, is that it has occurred precisely at a time when most criminologists state that public and political views towards law breaking and offenders have toughened up. As Garland (2001) and O'Malley (1999) argue, the interest in RJ represents the 'volatile' and often 'contradictory' range of recent developments in criminal justice. Global developments such as mandatory sentencing, 'three strike' legislation, 'zero tolerance' policing and the growth of extra judicial punishment in England and Wales (such as anti-social behaviour orders, spot fines and control orders) sit uneasily with an RJ approach that seeks to repair wounds and restore relationships in non-punitive and non-harmful ways.

The promise of RJ centres on a number of key values and positions. First, RJ affords victims and communities a major role in dealing with crime and conflict in society. According to proponents, RJ programmes deliberately place the offender and the victim at the centre of any restorative intervention in marked comparison to the marginal role afforded in our professionalised and bureaucratic criminal justice systems. The shortcomings were perhaps best highlighted by Nils Christie in his seminal lecture and subsequent paper, 'Conflicts as property' (Christie, 1977). Here Christie challenges our conceptualisation of the need for a professionalised criminal justice system, critiquing its propensity to steal the conflicts of the main protagonists – the victim and offender. By demonstrating how conflict and harm between people is transformed into crime against the state, Christie highlights how victims' participation and wishes are marginalised in the criminal justice process and their conflicts stolen by the state and its actors, lawyers and judges. Christie typifies the process as one in which:

> Firstly, the parties are being *represented*. Secondly, the one party that is being represented by the state, namely the victim, is so thoroughly represented that she or he for the most of the proceedings is pushed completely out of the arena, reduced to the triggerer-off of the whole thing. (1977, p 3, emphasis in original)

The victim therefore doubly loses, first as a result of being victimised by the offender and second, in having their participation and wishes 'stolen' by the state and professional criminal justice 'thieves' in the form of judges, lawyers and prosecutors. It is these professionals who decide on how the prosecution or trial is to proceed, which evidence is admissible and how the offender is to be punished. For Christie, the solution to growing criticisms of the criminal justice system's failure to account for the wishes and demands of victim groups and its inability to administer effective and publicly acceptable punishments lay in the revival of informal communitarian traditions where the victim and the offender play a full and active role in the response to harm and crime.

Moving on from RJ as a critique (and alternative) to the existing professionalised criminal justice system, the second promise of RJ is in its ability to deal with harm and crime in a different way. It is argued that a retributivist criminal justice system administers more harm and pain, whereas an RJ approach helps foster greater understanding between offender and victim in ways that repair hurt and harm and move both offender and victim on in their future lives. This links to further critiques of existing adversarial criminal justice systems that pit offender and victim against one another, with a response to harm that focuses on repairing the harm rather than punishing the offender. Zehr's *Changing Lens* is one of the foremost texts that propounds a rather different approach to harm and law breaking than we find in adversarial systems. For Zehr (1990), RJ offers alternative values in dealing with crime that contrast sharply with retribution. In his alternative lens, crime is defined by harm to people and to relationships in society, and the response to such harm moves away from the administration of further harms through punishment, vengeance and retaliation.

This value of *personalism* rather than *legalism* is inherent in a range of RJ conceptualisations. Personalism is also referred to in a range of other RJ values. Advocates speak of 'reconciliation' – encounters between victim and offender – as an alternative critique to the professionalised justice system. Personalism recognises a fundamental starting point for RJ advocates in that for them crime is essentially a violation of people, families and human relationships rather than merely the violation of a law. Hence, crime is not an abstract concept couched in legal language but rather behaviour which has a directly harmful impact on victims and the community (Roche, 2003). As such, the values by which personalism is enacted are important and Braithwaite and Parker (1999) have discussed how respect and equality are central in any encounter between those harmed and the perpetrator. This, in turn, has been termed non-domination. For example, the legislation that created the Truth and Reconciliation Council in post-Apartheid South Africa stated that in response to atrocities committed by both state and opposition groups:

> There is a need for understanding but not for vengeance, a need for
> reparation but not for retaliation, a need for humanity for others but not for
> victimization. (Roche, 2007, p 78)

As such, RJ offers a new value base that focuses on making amends or reparation to the victim by the offender. Furthermore, the restorative value of *reparation*, often by the offering of an apology that demonstrates that the offender both recognises and owns the harm caused to the victim is viewed as essential for repairing the physical and emotional harm caused to the victim. Reparation has a number of values closely associated with it. It is often referred to when authors discuss the centrality of 'making amends' or offering an apology to seek reconciliation. RJ therefore aims to heal the harm and rupture between the harmed and the harmer as well as strengthen the position and participation in society of both parties.

Another characteristic of RJ is that it encourages *reintegration*. Advocates of RJ also emphasise that the ideal does not solely operate for the benefit of victims of crime at the expense of offenders. Rather, offenders themselves are seen as benefiting from engagement with RJ practices (Braithwaite, 1989). Offenders can begin to be reintegrated back into their communities once they experience feelings of shame and remorse for their behaviour and ask for forgiveness from those they have hurt. Braithwaite does not advocate a shaming process that stigmatises people and keeps them as an excluded 'other' in society, but rather a process that focuses on the harmful behaviour of individuals and enables them to move on and seek a way forward to a law-abiding future. Perhaps more radical still, RJ discusses the possibility of forgiveness from the victim as a fundamental way of repairing the rupture between the two parties.

As a result, RJ offers roles to both offenders and the community in assuring that reintegration is best served. By offering a commitment to behave in a non-harmful way and make amends, offenders identify themselves with the norms of the law-abiding community. By offering forgiveness, the community symbolically welcomes the offender as accepted and included within the community (Roche, 2003, p 29).

Conceptualisations of restorative justice

Despite a vast amount of academic literature on restorative justice, a major growth in its use and an increasing focus on the issue by the United Nations and by a variety of different consortia and umbrella organisations of RJ activists it remains a difficult task to define what we mean by restorative justice. It remains a term of conceptual ambiguity, characterised by lack of clarity 'often seen as complicated and confused', as perplexing and consisting of a 'mixed ideological bag' (Daly and Immarigeon, 1998, p 21). It is easier to consider what restorative justice is not (that is, deliberately hurtful) or begin to deconstruct it by discussing its constituent parts or the variety of processes such as victim–offender mediation or scripted conferences. However, it can be argued that in doing so we cast our gaze away from difficult yet fundamental considerations regarding conceptualising restorative justice.

As Gavrielides (2009) acknowledges, the conceptual plurality of RJ is related not only to definitional issues and the extent of the shelter of the RJ umbrella, but also to a multiplicity of proponents, interest groups, academics, RJ trainers, researchers and funding streams and their respective hopes and futures for RJ. Much of the perplexing nature of the RJ concept arises out of conflicts or 'fault lines' (Gavrielides,

2008). Perhaps the most fundamental tension in conceptualising RJ, and one that has enormous impact on how it is used and what outcomes we might expect it to produce, comes from tensions between whether or not we see RJ as a radical transformative 'replacing' discourse to existing criminal justice. Here restorative justice is conceptualised as an alternative paradigm to the retributivist and professionalised criminal justice system, based on repairing the wounds in human relationships through making amends and offering forgiveness (Zehr, 1990) and an approach that breaks with the formalised and professionalised system of dealing with harm (Christie, 1977). As such, RJ is considered to be a replacement to a system that focuses on breaking the rules of law and seeks an outcome that punishes the perpetrator. The tension here is with another discourse that views RJ approaches in much more pragmatic terms. In this view, RJ is conceptualised as a complementary set of practices that can be made to run alongside the criminal justice system or indeed be a reforming part of it. As such, in England and Wales we have seen the advent of reparation as part of the referral order. As a result, RJ becomes merely one of a range of criminal justice approaches or tools for the criminal justice professional.

These conceptual tensions have therefore led to a multiplicity of visions of restorative justice. These are summarised usefully by the questions raised by Gavrielides (2008):

- Should RJ be outside or inside the existing criminal justice system?
- Should RJ be defined principally by alternative processes to dealing with crime or by achieving alternative restorative outcomes?
- Is RJ an alternative to being punished or can it usefully be co-opted as a more humane and emotionally intelligent form of punishment that offers sentencers a different and creative alternative to punitivism?
- Finally, how 'pure' should the values of RJ be and can they be flexibly applied?

Such tensions are important considerations for advocates of RJ to consider. They relate directly to key considerations relevant to our research in children's residential care, considerations such as whether children should be coerced into discussing their harmful behaviour and the impact it has on others. The answer to this question follows on from whether we view RJ as a form of punishment or as a meaningful and consensual process in which individuals participate voluntarily. Other considerations include whether children who have been harmed should be able to refuse to offer the perpetrator the chance to discuss their behaviour with them, where RJ is the preferred method of dealing with harmful behaviour in a residential home. Furthermore, the issue of whether RJ is an alternative paradigm to the existing criminal justice system leads to consideration of the roles and responsibilities of those involved in the delivery of RJ initiatives. In the children's homes visited for the purposes of this research, independent facilitators were not available in RJ encounters. Finally, the question of whether restorative justice is a fluid or a 'pure' concept creates tensions when the portability of RJ is considered and its reach extended to new arenas such as residential childcare. Proponents have to ask which of the main values, processes and outcomes – for example, voluntarism, the encounter (that is, the meeting of parties involved) and reintegration – are required to be present and which can be melded or disregarded and remain a powerful restorative intervention. Without a resolution to these tensions or at least a consideration of them, RJ will remain a perplexing concept and its ability to offer creative and effective responses to crime and harmful behaviour could be detrimentally affected. RJ can therefore mean a transformative model or ethical stance to crime and harm in society, for example, a chance meeting and sharing of views between two pupils in conflict in the school corridor (Morrison, 2001) or a situation where the police avoid charging and processing a young person through the criminal justice system.

Practices and outcomes of restorative justice

In discussing and making sense of the phenomenon of RJ, authors have focused on two aspects. First, much attention has been afforded to the processes of restorative justice, that is, the ways and methods by which RJ can be delivered. Although restorative practices and outcomes are interrelated, they have often been discussed in isolation or at best as alternative approaches to the implementation of RJ. Marshall's (1999) definition of RJ is an exemplar of the 'process' and 'purist' notion of restorative justice:

> ... a process whereby all the parties with a stake in a particular offence come together to resolve collectively how to deal with the aftermath of the offence and its implications for the future. (p 36)

This definition focuses on the processes of conflict resolution with all parties empowered to play in a collective agreement for the future. In practice, the process model of RJ has led to a number of innovative approaches to a range of encounters between victim and offender, such as victim–offender mediation programmes and wider conferences where interested parties are also included in the discussions and future plans (for example, family group conferences (FGCs). Raye and Roberts (2007) offer a number of variations on these themes with processes involving what they term 'shuttle diplomacy', whereby victims and offenders communicate through an intermediary or trained mediator. The role of the mediator is to pass on communication, act as an intermediary between the two parties in a form of indirect encounter. Here the identification of a victim or person harmed is clearly fundamental to the operation of direct encounter. Without this, there can be no dialogue with the offender. Conferencing, in particular FGCs, originated in New Zealand and moved quickly to the district of Wagga Wagga in New South Wales, Australia, soon becoming an example of policy transference to England and Wales. The inclusion of family members and other supporters of the victim and offender has emerged as a powerful example of RJ, particularly in relation to child welfare and youth crime (Hayden, 2007, 2009). There have also emerged less formalised, more fluid, models of restorative justice. The requirement for a conference to have a formal script and a formalised allocation of roles has been adapted to other environments. In the context of using RJ in schools, Morrison (2001) has coined the term 'corridor conferencing' or 'stand-up RJ' to encompass a method of communicating about harm and enabling offenders to make amends within the educational setting that emphasises informality, speed and the impromptu nature of such an approach. Clearly, in a school environment, corridor conferencing, which allows most problems to be dealt with there and then, has the benefit of immediacy compared with the rather elaborate (and expensive) arrangements required to have a formalised FGC with family members, an independent facilitator, a neutral venue and catering facilities. Indeed, in schools, restorative *justice* may become restorative *approach* and is often used as part of the behaviour management system (Morrison, 2001).

Perhaps the most helpful way of capturing the varieties of processes or practices in the RJ 'umbrella' is Wachtel's (1999) continuum of practices, illustrated in Figure 1.1. This response to wrongdoing enables RJ to be considered along a continuum, starting with a way of making statements or asking questions that effect a response from the offender and enables them to consider the impact of their behaviour on others. In our research into the implementation of an RJ approach in children's residential care, asking the child questions such as 'How do you think [child's name] felt when you took their pocket money?' were used to move children from considering their own needs to those of others. A little more formality was apparent when a staff member took children to one side and asked them questions about their behaviour and allowed the victim to communicate their feelings. In the continuum, these small impromptu conferences involved direct participation and 'encounter' between offender and victim, but without the need for a formal script or outside mediation.

Figure 1.1: Restorative practices continuum

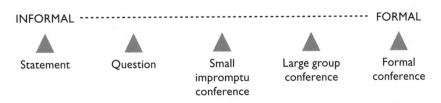

Statement	eg staff member to young person: 'You really hurt John's feelings when you did that.'
Question	eg staff member to young person: 'How do you think Jane felt when you did that?'
Small impromptu conference	eg between member of staff and two young people in a dispute or situation
Large group	eg between member(s) of staff, people from outside the home (such conference as a neighbour), several young people (or all those resident)
Formal conference	ie to include formal invitations to people from outside the home. Formally scripted conference (as per training)

Source: Based on Wachtel, 1999, p 3

A focus on restorative outcomes has arisen partially from the development in notions of RJ that have focused on processes or changes to what you do to respond to crime or harmful behaviour. Critics of the process-based models argue that RJ advocates and researchers can, if one is not careful, adopt a rather incomplete understanding of the RJ phenomenon because restorative outcomes are absent from our considerations. A consideration of *why* one works in a restorative way and *what* end results can be achieved is fundamental to ensuring that harmful behaviour is meaningfully addressed. Restorative justice outcomes such as reparation, apology, forgiveness and reintegration are important to consider in conjunction with the alternative processes of dealing with harmful behaviour. As a result, in our research it was important for staff and children to encapsulate RJ as both an alternative way of dealing with harmful behaviour, conflict and crime and an alternative ending to a problem, which involved saying sorry, doing something to make amends and feeling part of the children's home 'community'. Such a difficult melding of restorative processes and outcomes was essential in residential care to ensure that children were not offered restorative processes to discuss problematic behaviour only for the 'offender' to receive the traditional punishments of being fined, sent to bed or subjected to a range of 'loss of' privileges or services (see Chapter Seven). Moreover, a focus on a fluid understanding of 'encounter' and 'communication' enabled victims to have their feelings and wishes aired in the homes, rather than the residential care staff merely demanding apologies from offenders.

The melding of restorative process and outcomes is best illustrated in all its complexity by Daniel Van Ness' (2002) thoughts on a framework for assessing RJ. Van Ness (2002) configures a framework that allows for the key process and outcome features to be included under four values – encounter, amends, reintegration and inclusion. Van Ness (2002) skilfully allows for a meeting of the parties concerned, respectful communication between those involved in conflict, agreement for a way forward, the making of amends by offender to the victim, the changing of behaviour by the offender for the future, the provision of assistance to victim and offender and the inclusion of both parties in the future (Van Ness, 2002, p 6).

The effectiveness of restorative justice

Attention given to RJ outcomes in recent years has led to meta-analyses and systematic reviews of research evidence. In an era of evidence-based practice and a search for 'what works' in ways to combat crime and anti-social behaviour, RJ's fundamental promise has moved from being an inclusive approach to both victims and offenders, whereby both parties are placed to the centre of the approach, to an increased focus on offenders. Although concern over improving victim satisfaction with RJ intervention remains strong, governments and policy makers have turned their attention to RJ's transformative effects on offenders themselves in terms of reducing recidivism (Robinson and Shapland, 2008, p 337). More recently, we have seen a plethora of evaluative studies that have analysed reconviction data following an RJ intervention. This culminated in Sherman and Strang's (2007) systematic review; hence an interest in the wider contribution of RJ in reducing recidivism within the criminal justice system. Here the conceptualisation of RJ is as a rehabilitative process for offenders faced with the realities of their behaviour as outlined by the victims themselves. Offenders are 'restored', in Braithwaite's words, or rehabilitated, by becoming changed and empathetic after hearing about the full impact of their harmful behaviour on others in an encounter with the victim. In addition, these tests of effectiveness for RJ move away from less easily measured outcomes such as 'restoring victims' or 'making state care a better place for children' and influence what organisations want or expect from using an RJ approach. However, what organisations 'want' or 'expect' from implementing RJ can be strongly influenced by simplistic performance management measures, as monitored by central government.

Figure 1.2: Restorative justice as a whole-system approach

	Encounter	Amends	Reintegration	Inclusion
	Meeting, communication and agreement	Apology, restitution and change	Respect and assistance	Invitation, acknowledgement of interests, acceptance of alternative approaches
	Meeting and communication	Apology and restitution	Respect	Invitation and acknowledgement of interests
More	Meeting and agreement	Apology and change	Assistance	Invitation
	Communication and agreement	Restitution and change	Indifference to either victim or offender	Traditional participation
	Communication	Apology	Indifference to both victim and offender	No interest in participation of parties
	Agreement	Restitution	Stigmatisation of either victim or offender	Prevention of parties' participation
Less	No encounter	Change	Stigmatisation or isolation of both victim and offender	Prevention of parties who want to observe
	Separation of parties	No amends or new harm	Safety obtained through separation	Coercion of unwilling parties

Source: Based on Van Ness, 2002, p 20

Sherman and Strang (2007) found that restorative justice works differently at different times with different people. Indeed, some of their evidence should enable a reconsideration of the applicability of RJ with offender populations. First, Sherman and Strang (2007) found that RJ approaches could make substantial inroads into recidivism rates for both property and violent crime. Second, Sherman and Strang's analysis found that RJ seems to have a better treatment effect with *more* rather than less serious crimes. In particular, the approach worked better with crimes where there was a personal victim. As such, the use of RJ with violent crime was deemed to be a fruitful approach. Of particular interest here, in relation to the overrepresentation of looked after children in the criminal justice system, is Sherman and Strang's (2007) analysis of the Canberra Reintegrative Shaming Experiments programmes for young people where encounters with the victims were arranged as an alternative to prosecution. Their findings show that RJ-assigned young people had 84 fewer arrests for violent crime per 100 offenders per year than those who were prosecuted and processed through the youth justice system (Sherman and Strang, 2007, p 16).

More food for thought regarding the effectiveness of restorative justice can be found in Robinson and Shapland's (2008) research for the Home Office Crime Reduction Programme in England and Wales. In evidencing the reduction of recidivism, the authors analysed three schemes involving adult and youth offenders. Robinson and Shapland (2008) turn their attention to uncovering *why* RJ has worked and surmise that it is the process of maximising offenders' emotional literacy in being able to hear and process internally the harmful nature of their behaviour. They use Braithwaite's idea of 'reintegrative shaming' to examine the transformative potential of RJ in the offender. Reintegrative shaming has been characterised as:

> ... the disapproval dispensed within an ongoing relationship with the offender of respect, whereby shame induces guilt rather than techniques of neutralisation over the offender deeds. (Braithwaite, 1989, p 72)

An earlier meta-analyses by Latimer et al (2001) was less positive about the impact on recidivism, but positive (as most studies are) about victim and offender satisfaction within the RJ process:

> The addition of restorative justice programmes has enhanced victim satisfaction in a process that was, by its very nature, rather unsatisfactory. Moreover, this response to criminal behaviour has a strong impact by encouraging more offenders to take responsibility for their actions and repair through restitution some of the harm they have caused. And while the gains made in recidivism are not as strong as 'appropriate correctional treatment', restorative justice does appear to reduce recidivism for those who chose to participate. Finally, offenders in restorative justice programmes report moderate increases in satisfaction compared to offenders in traditional systems. (p 23)

Robinson and Shapland (2008) use Bazemore's (1998) work to further elaborate on how RJ can reduce recidivism by focusing on the experiences of victims and offenders. The authors consider reparative work to the victim, or the community in general, to be of central significance towards a feeling of inclusion, belonging and reintegration for offenders and the development of social capital. Finally, RJ is seen to have an important contribution in the development of cognitive and emotional processes involved in giving up criminal behaviour. By enabling offenders to assert guilt and remorse in an encounter with a victim before planning to move on, restorative justice can offer offenders the mechanism to begin to create alternative self-perception, identities and productive and law-abiding ways of living.

The new focus on the power of R to reduce recidivism and transform those involved in its variety of approaches has led Sherman and Strang (2007) to assert that:

> ... there is far more evidence on RJ, with more positive results, than there has been for most innovations in criminal justice that have ever been rolled out in the country. (p 8)

However, the danger here for RJ advocates is in the increasingly utilitarian ways in which RJ has been tested. By incorporating RJ into wider evaluations of 'what works' with offenders, there is a sense that the value-driven approach of RJ may be lost to a powerful crime reduction agenda. While crime reduction through offenders transforming their behaviour is a welcome consequence of RJ interventions, it differs from the treatment or rehabilitation paradigms in that reductions in offending behaviour can only be achieved in so far as the victims' needs and wishes remain centre stage.

Restorative youth justice in England and Wales

In England and Wales, the impact of RJ has arguably been felt most forcefully in the profound and unprecedented changes that have occurred in the field of youth justice. Elements of 'restoration' to victims and communities as new youth justice practice were first found in New Labour's flagship 1998 Crime and Disorder Act. As part of the move to the increased 'responsibilisation' of organisations in relation to crime control, the government created multi-agency youth offending teams and placed restoration to the victim or community as a central plank of their practice. The 1998 Act also heralded the introduction of action plan orders and reparation orders, which, while short-lived, benchmarked the notion of making amends and encounters with victims and communities into the systematically changed youth justice system. The 1999 Youth Justice and Criminal Evidence Act was important in terms of mainstreaming RJ into the youth justice system in England and Wales. A central part of the Act was the creation of the referral order (Crawford and Newburn, 2003). Referral orders are essentially a 'mandatory standard sentence' (Muncie and Goldson, 2006, p 42) imposed on all offenders between 10 and 17 years of age who have pleaded guilty and have no previous convictions.

After evaluation of their use in 11 pilot areas, referral orders were used nationally from 2002. The key here for our purposes is the practice of referring young offenders to a youth offender panel made up of local volunteers in an informal environment to make and agree arrangements for a future plan to reduce recidivism. The Act allows the possibility of making referral orders of three to 12 months' duration. The plan agreed by the youth offender panel and the offender can include direct or indirect victim reparation, an encounter with the victim through mediation services, curfew provisions, exclusion from certain places and persons, and participation in activities designed to have an impact on the offender's 'risk factors', which are believed to lead to their criminal behaviour. As such, the referral order reflects a hybridisation of inclusionary and reparative ethos with controlling and exclusionary sentiments. The order's core aims are therefore to provide first-time entrants into the courts the:

> ... opportunity to make restoration to the victim, take responsibility for the consequences of their offending and achieve integration into the law abiding community. (Haines and O'Mahony, 2006, p 112)

Notably, referral order panels are comprised of two community members with a youth offending team professional encapsulating a real communitarian approach to dealing with youth crime. Furthermore, the victim can attend the panel meeting to voice their feelings and wishes and meet the offender in an *encounter* (Haines and O'Mahony, 2006, p 113).

These arrangements capture a changing professional value system in youth justice. New Labour dissolved the previous youth justice teams with their associated ethos of diverting young people from the youth justice system wherever possible and replaced them with the multi-agency youth offending teams and their approach of 'early intervention' in the lives of young people 'at risk' or on the borders of criminal behaviour. As such, the final warning and referral order schemes for all first-time offenders reflect a desire for professional intervention rather than a willingness to divert (Goldson, 2000). Within the youth justice system, therefore, RJ in recent years can be seen to be an idea whose time has come.

Restorative justice, civil society and residential childcare

As Strang and Braithwaite (2001) state in their highly influential book *Restorative Justice and Civil Society*, both RJ and civil society are hot topics for social scientists. Here, they use civil society in a broad context, referring to it as any institution between the state and the individual. As such, it encapsulates families, churches, workplaces, schools and notions of community (Strang and Braithwaite, 2001, p 1). Understanding the contribution of restorative justice in improving communities, workplaces and families breaks free from a conceptualisation of the phenomenon as an alternative to an adversarial criminal justice system or an additional tool within it. It introduces notions of improvements in 'everyday life', between individuals and ultimately a better way of living life in a democracy'. A reconfiguration of RJ as a problem-solving, democratic and empowering way for individuals, families and communities to deal with conflicts rather than respond to crime allows for a much greater and more expansive involvement of restorative values in society. In this conceptualisation, the relevance of RJ for everyday life invokes a 'grander project of enhancing the civility of society' (Wachtel and McCold, 2001, p 114).

The introduction of RJ within the children's social care arena is an example of RJ being utilised more broadly to mould and strengthen standards of appropriate behaviour between children and adults in the care system. The research we outline here therefore has relevancy in two respects. First, RJ can be used as a paradigm to respond to law breaking by children; specifically, RJ approaches and values can be adopted with the aim of reducing the criminalisation of children and young people in care. Encounters between victim and offender can be adopted as an alternative to police involvement and a criminal justice response. Second, and more broadly, restorative justice could have a role to play in improving the care experience through greater (respectful) communication between individuals, the sharing of feelings and wishes and the non-punitive resolution of conflict through the direct involvement of the protagonists. As a result, this research into RJ approaches in children's residential care has relevancy for those interested in RJ's impact in both criminal justice and civil society, studying as it does children in care who are overrepresented in the offending statistics. To some degree, the use of RJ as a way of challenging the overrepresentation of looked after young people in the criminal justice system goes against the contemporary reliance on professional interventionism into the lives of 'at risk' young people. An RJ approach would tend to preclude the involvement of the state and highlight the resolution of harmful behaviour within the community of those involved. In the research reported in this volume, the spotlight is on the protagonists and the community in the children's home. The crime reduction charity Nacro (2003) highlights the possibility that:

> ... the use of restorative justice techniques may well provide a course of action to resolve incidents, with the appropriate recognition of the interests of all involved and without the need to seek recourse through the formal criminal justice system. (p 37)

The local authority at the centre of this study implemented an RJ approach for a number of reasons, one of which was to reduce perceived reliance on the police and outside authorities such as out-of-hours teams to deal with conflict or harmful behaviour. As a result, it was hoped that an RJ approach and associated values would enable the homes to undertake organisational change and 'own their own conflicts' in a similar way to families, in a manner reminiscent of Christie's ideal (Christie, 1977). While restorative justice within the residential childcare environment remains one of the least researched, evaluated and written about areas of practice, there has been a growing interest in its use in this context.

The local authority also adopted restorative approaches as the key to improving the nature of relationships between children and staff in care homes, and between the children themselves. The restorative values of taking responsibility for one's actions, dealing with conflicts by communication between the protagonists and direct involvement in the solutions to harmful behaviour were all part of the RJ implemented. This envisaged a professional move in the care homes away from dealing with conflict or harmful behaviour by 'fines', such as the delaying of pocket money, early bedtimes and withdrawing access to TV, games machines and the pool table (usually described by staff and children in the research as 'loss of' a range of valued items). As such, the 'transformative potential' of RJ was harnessed to 'community build' (White, 2003) or make improvements in everyday 'family life' within the children's homes (Törrönen, 2006) in order to foster a sense of belonging, respect, care, inclusion and ownership.

When the research started (2006), only one small-scale study on the use of RJ in children's residential care was identified. This research was undertaken in Hertfordshire (Littlechild, 2003) and focused on one residential unit. The research showed a reduction in the rate of police call-outs of 22% over a 10-month period. There was also a reduction in incidents in which 'alternative measures of control' (such as physical restraint) were used; these decreased by 54%. Thus police call-outs and incident reports were seen as related to and indicative of the use of RJ. Both measures are within the control of staff in how they respond to conflict. Importantly, there was an *increase* in the number of incidents of violence in the residential unit during the period of Littlechild's (2003) research. This was explained by the admission of one young person after RJ measures had been implemented and this individual was excluded when it came to the overall positive conclusion in the report on the impact of the RJ approach. This highlights the problem of non-representation when researching small numbers in residential care units, as well as the difficulties of inference and interpretation of such research. Individual children with challenging behaviour are a feature of the residential care environment and any RJ measures need to address their needs as well as those of the children who present less of a challenge; alternatively, the limits of an RJ approach should be recognised. Overall Littlechild's (2003) evaluation concluded that RJ had been implemented successfully, leading to a transformation in staff practices and a lesser change in children's attitudes and behaviour.

During the course of the current research, Willmott (2007) conducted a 'scoping review' (for the National Children's Bureau) of the use of RJ in children's residential care. This consisted of a literature search and 13 telephone discussions and contacts with representatives from a range of projects. The review identified 10 schemes in operation and three about to start. Willmott found that the majority of RJ programmes in residential care were recent, typically starting in 2004 or later, and that 'there are currently no formal evaluations of these programmes' (p 8). In general, RJ was being used in children's residential care to:

- reduce offending rates and the potential for criminalising young people in residential care;
- provide an alternative way of dealing with non-criminal harm or conflict within residential settings;
- provide a different approach to behaviour management.

The techniques used ranged from conferencing between protagonists and a trained mediator or member of staff, informal discussions or meetings and individual reparative discussions, reflecting the continuum of restorative practices in Figure 1.1.

Hopkins (2008), in her review of restorative approaches in residential childcare, discusses the underpinning principles and value base in relation to what is known about effective practice in residential childcare. She argues that restorative approaches empower all those involved and lead to improved relationships between staff and young people, to include the development of mutual respect, active listening to one another and the creation of a child-centred institution. However, Hopkins also reminds us that staff cultures take time to change and that training in a new approach is only a first step.

In sum, the available research evidence about RJ is relatively positive but the more authoritative and impartial work of Sherman and Strang (2007) reminds us to look more closely at *with whom* and *how* it is used. At the time of writing, there is no larger-scale research on the use of RJ in children's residential care. The current study is an attempt to investigate how a particular RJ approach was implemented and with what impact, across 10 children's residential care homes in one local authority.

2

Children in care: the policy context

Introduction

Having reviewed in Chapter One debates and evidence about restorative justice (RJ) as a response to conflict and offending behaviour, this chapter sets out to consider the particular setting in which this approach was applied in the current research. What is specific to this setting is the focus on children and young people in residential care. This chapter sets out to present the evolving policy context for children in care more broadly (as children move between different forms of care), connecting the circumstances of coming into care, or being in care, with the behaviours that might be addressed by using an RJ approach. The chapter starts with a brief look at the origins of the care system and how this relates to poverty, vulnerability and social exclusion, and how this interconnects with conflict and offending behaviour. The concept of 'managing risk' is introduced in relation to these circumstances and behaviours, within the broader policy discourse about risk. Evidence about a range of relevant 'outcomes' from the care experience is presented and discussed. The contemporary focus on improving outcomes from care through the Care Matters White Paper (DCSF, 2006), within the overall framework of Every Child Matters (DCSF, 2003), is outlined.

Children in care: poverty, marginalisation and social exclusion

In trying to understand how and why the care system has evolved and the nature of the behavioural issues presented to, and managed by, staff and carers, it is worth briefly considering the historical backdrop from which the current system has developed and continues to evolve. There is historical evidence that some children have always been brought up or lived for extended periods outside their birth families (Gorin, 2000). Some have lived away from 'home' or birth parents for a period, often with relatives or family friends. Others have been sent away to boarding schools. These different reasons for living away from home are qualitatively different, particularly in relation to any degree of adult choice exercised, the reasons for any choice or decision and the extent to which officialdom or the state is involved, if at all. Also there are likely to be differences in the way behaviours are managed in residential (or group) settings in comparison with individual family homes that act as foster carers. There are practical possibilities and strategies that are more (or less) relevant in these different settings. However, for much of human history, these arrangements have not been governed by the state and 'childhood' as a stage in life did not have the same meaning in the past as it does today. Therefore, in understanding the background history to children in care, it is important to consider a number of key themes in relation to social policy and childhood.

In relation to the concept of 'childhood' and children as potentially vulnerable, there is the well-known view put forward by Aries (1960) that there was no separate social space for 'childhood' prior to the middle ages. According to Aries, 'childhood' is seen as developing in the 16th and 17th centuries among the professional and property-owning classes. Although this picture of the past may have been overstated, it does remind us that our expectations and conceptions of childhood are related to socioeconomic circumstances and the way a society organises and looks after its most vulnerable members. Frost and Stein (1989) argue that feudal society served orphaned and illegitimate children relatively well, through a system of social obligations that underpinned the placement and boarding of children. However, this sense of obligation happened alongside moral taboos and stigma about the family of origin of these children. In Britain, the Poor Law of 1563 was the first formal recognition of any state responsibility towards poor children who could not be maintained by their family, or who were orphaned (Cameron and Maginn, 2009). The emphasis was on putting children to work. These provisions reflected wider concerns about destitution and vagrancy. They also reflected a developing rationale regarding the social benefits of morally educating the children of the poor. A key principle of the Poor Law and the associated workhouse system was that of 'less eligibility'. This principle was based on the belief that those in the workhouse experienced conditions worse than those outside. The 1834 Poor Law Amendment Act led to a partial shift to 'indoor' industrial training in buildings separate from workhouses, but was not greatly dissimilar to the earlier legislation. Cameron and Maginn (2009) remind us that until the rise of an industrial Britain in the 18th century poor children died in large numbers from malnutrition, disease, negligence and abuse unless they went into 'the workhouse' or were looked after by the philanthropy of their local community or the church.

Poverty and destitution is therefore the key backdrop to the origins of state intervention in the lives of children. Another explicit reason for state provision is an understanding of the connection between poverty and delinquent or criminal behaviour. Concerns about child welfare came later, developing in the 19th century. In the mid-19th century, Mary Carpenter argued that an undisciplined childhood, lacking in moral or religious influence, was one of the chief causes of juvenile delinquency. She distinguished between two broad groups of children – the 'dangerous' and the 'perishing' classes. The latter were those who were 'at risk', as opposed to being already involved in crime. The 'perishing classes' were the 'children of misfortune, their parents either dead or careless, vicious and abandoned: their homes if they have any, comfortless and wretched; their dress ragged and insufficient' (O'Leary of Manchester, 1856, quoted in Smith, 1998, p 20). Then, as now, it was often argued by reformers that it was the duty of the better elements in society to rescue such children from their misfortune and the likelihood of getting into more and more serious trouble. By the latter part of the 19h century, childcare charities were established: National Children's Homes (1869), Barnardo's (1870), the Church of England Waifs and Strays Society (1881), the National Society for the Prevention and Cruelty to Children (1884) and the Catholic Children's Society (1887). Cruelty to children became a criminal offence in 1889.

Poverty (and the misfortunes associated with it) was key to *why* some children came into care a few decades ago. Rowlands and Statham (2009) argue that many children who came into care during the 1950s, 1960s and 1970s came from loving families who could not care for their children because of unemployment, homelessness, illness and so on. In contemporary society, the emphasis is on keeping (or returning) children to their birth family or wider family network (through kinship care where possible). This means that by the time children come into the care system today, many are already in a situation in which no-one cares for them unconditionally in a parental role. Most will still have extended family members, but a minority will not. In essence, many children in care do not have adults they can rely on to stand by them and plan on their behalf. It is difficult to overestimate the disadvantage of this situation, which has been viewed as one of the most significant factors in the process of social exclusion (White, 2008). The extent to which processes and provisions in the care system can address this situation is hampered by the lack of placement choice that bedevils the system. Lack of choice means that placements cannot always provide for a child's needs; in turn, this can lead to placement breakdown and the associated upset, disruption and sense of rejection and failure. Nationally, 10.7% (DCSF, 2009b) of children in care for a year or more experience three or more placements. Movements in placement can disrupt friendships and may mean moving schools or having to make long taxi journeys to school. All in all, the current system operates in such a way that it inadvertently enhances the possibilities of social exclusion for some children rather than combats the existing problem. Axford (2010) notes that this concept of social exclusion has a high profile in contemporary children's services in Britain, with particular emphasis being given to those who are 'multiply disadvantaged', such as children in care.

More generally, social exclusion as a concept has been much used (and misused) in policy discourse in Britain since the mid-1990s. Any focus on children in care is just one part of this debate. In short, the concept offers a general metaphor that is understood to describe the set of circumstances that people may face in poorer areas – such as unemployment, poor housing, high crime levels, poor health, high levels of family breakdown, a low skill base and low incomes for those in work. Although MacDonald and Marsh (2001) are critical of the concept of social exclusion, saying that its meaning remains open to interpretation, they nevertheless state that they believe that it is of some worth because of its emphasis on processes and how circumstances operate over time and also because locality is recognised as important. Young (2002) is also critical, warning of the dangers of using this concept in that it can carry with it a series of false binaries, ignoring the problems of the included majority. So while problems may well be concentrated in particular areas, locations or social groups, they are not exclusive to them. It is worth considering these criticisms when using the concept of social exclusion in relation to children in care. First, it is important to emphasise that not all children in care should be seen as 'socially excluded'; some are in stable placements and some also achieve at school and beyond. Second, there are important differences across the care experience, not least because of the major differences between placement types, such as residential, kinship and foster care.

Alongside social exclusion, other popular policy discourses are applied in particular ways to children in care, in particular the concept of risk. This concept operates on a number of levels, including the broader discourse on risk and society as well as one in which children in care both pose risks to others or are themselves 'at risk' because of their vulnerability. This 'at risk' status tends, like social exclusion, to be used as a metaphor for problematic outcomes, as in 'at risk of social exclusion', 'at risk of placement breakdown', 'at risk of criminal involvement' and so on. Young people in the care system are then 'risk assessed', after which they may be categorised as low, medium or high 'risk'. Yet this risk is multifaceted and can be poorly articulated. Furthermore, comparative risk is not well understood, for example, the risk of being left with abusive parents compared with the risks associated with the care system. Ritchie (2005) notes that although taking children into care is a way of ensuring their safety, there is no systematic research or data collection on the institutional abuse of children or any evaluation of the risk of significant harm within care. We do know something about the prevalence of certain experiences within care, such as bullying, physical and sexual assault, but there are rarely any meaningful comparisons made relevant to the alternatives facing these children. We do know from child abuse enquiries, however, that children abused within foster or residential care settings do not necessarily report it or have their concerns forwarded to those who can do something about it (Waterhouse et al, 2000).

The association between having to leave one's birth parents, the disruptions that can be experienced because of the way the care system operates, and behavioural problems, conflict and offending behaviour are well known (Hayden et al, 1999). These associations can lead to confusion in the public perception of *why* children are in care. Contemporary evidence shows that the great majority of children in care are there because of abuse, neglect or family problems. Only a small minority are there because of what they have done. Nevertheless, their experiences prior to care and in some care environments can make for more problematic and difficult to manage behaviour than in the general population of young people. In this sense, RJ is one of the more recent attempts to address a long-term need for behaviour management strategies, particularly within the residential care system.

Types of care placement

Residential children's homes, whether primarily for care or control, were a common response in the 19th and early 20th centuries. For example, Hendrick (1994) estimates that between 1900 and 1914, 70,000-80,000 children were in various forms of residential care under the Poor Law, while only about 10,000 were 'boarded out' to families willing to take them (p 76). It is interesting to note that a century later, a similar number of children to those provided for by the Poor Law, are now 'in care' for more than one year, although because of population increase this represents a smaller proportion of all children. Also, the balance of where children are cared for has changed totally over the past century, with most children now being cared for in families (through foster care) than in residential care (see Table 2.1).

Table 2.1 illustrates the proportion of children in different placement types in March 2009. Nearly three quarters (73%) of children in care are placed with foster carers in the community; this proportion has continued to increase from around 40% of all placements in 1981 (see Hayden et al, 1999). A small proportion, 7% in 2009, live with their parents but are subject to supervision from social services. Residential placements, including secure accommodation, children's homes and hostels, account for 10% of placements (around 6,500 children). Some children are in other provisions, such as residential schools (3%) or other community settings (3%), and the rest are placed for adoption (4%).

The population in care is dynamic, with children moving between placements and placement types, as well as back home to birth parents or other family, as well as leaving the system when they are of age. Overall in England at any one time, children in care number around 60,000, although the total number of children who pass through the care system in a year is higher (over 90,000 children in a year). A smaller number

Table 2.1: Placement types of looked after children (2008-09)

Placement type	%
Foster care	73
Secure units, children's homes and hostels	10
With parents	7
Placed for adoption	4
Other (residential schools, lodgings, other residential settings)	3
Other placements in the community	3

Source: DCSF, 2009b

have been in care for at least a year (around 44,000 44-45,000 in most government monitoring reports) and of these, about three quarters are of school age. Around three quarters (73%) of children in care are White British, with the rest being of Black and Minority Ethnic origin (DCSF, 2009b). More boys (57%) than girls (43%) are in care (DCSF, 2009b). Despite the policy emphasis of keeping children with their birth parents wherever possible, the number and rate of children 'looked after' has stayed at a similar level for several years: 54 children in 10,000 (DCSF, 2009b).

By the early 1990s, it was clear that residential care for children was fast becoming a placement of 'last resort' throughout the European Union (Sellick, 1998). Sellick

(1998) argues that this has happened despite the needs of children, the limitations of foster care and the potential of residential services. The residential sector in England has been in decline for decades and has been the subject of numerous reviews and several high-profile scandals (as in North Wales) as well as investigations into abusive regimes such as 'pindown' (Kirkwood, 1993). Yet Stein (2006b, p 14) reminds us that the 'pindown' regime was accepted for a time as 'a solution to an intractable problem: the care and, more pertinently, the control of some of the most difficult young people in the care system'. Coldrey (2001) documents the widespread use of physical abuse as a way of trying to control the behaviour of young people in residential care until a few decades ago. Without doubt, these events have tarnished the reputation of the remaining homes and morale of staff working in the sector. Indeed, Clough and colleagues (2006, p 4) have argued that the marginalisation suffered by many in the care system is exacerbated in residential care by the tendency for residential staff to be 'excluded' even within children's services. They go on to explain that this is because the accepted orthodoxy is that foster placements are preferred.

Comparing 'outcomes': children leaving care and other children

There is a long history of research documenting the poor outcomes for children spending time in care, with residential care having the most negative image. Comparison between children in care and the general population of young people is now routinely available annually through government monitoring in Britain, as is research, and is a stark reminder of the massive contrast between the life chances of children in the care of the state and those who live at home. However, the data in Table 2.2 can be misleading because it is based on the whole population of children in care for more than a year; therefore, it masks the even more problematic circumstances of residential care.

At the time of writing, Table 2.2 illustrates the comparison on key indicators between children in care for more than a year and all children. Offending behaviour was the most important issue that the RJ approach was introduced to address in the current research; however, it was obvious to the case study local authority that in reality offending behaviour was not the main (or only) issue for most children engaged in behaviours that caused conflict. Indeed the interconnections between conflict and problematic behaviour, mental health problems, offending behaviour and poor educational outcomes and becoming 'NEET' (not in education, employment or training) are all too obvious and well appreciated in the case study local authority. We will deal in more depth with the evidence about offending behaviour and children in care in Chapter Four.

When trying to understand these disparities and why they might relate to how children behave, it is worth considering why children come into care and how the processes involved and different care environments might influence these disparities.

Nearly two thirds of children become known to social services because of abuse or neglect, and around half are admitted to care for this reason. A range of family

Table 2.2: Comparing key indicators for children in care with those of all children

Indicator	Children in care (%)	All children (%)
Offending behaviour: final warning or conviction[1]	9	4.3
Educational achievement: 5+ GCSEs, A*-C[1]	14	65
Excluded from school[1]	0.5	0.1
Special educational needs[1]	27.9	2.8
Unemployed: September after leaving school [1]	17	5
'NEET' at 19: not in education employment or training[2]	30	10
Mental health problems[2]	45	10

Sources: [1] DCSF, 2009a; [2] NCB, 2007

problems make up most of the rest of the other reasons, including child or parent illness. Only a minority of children are admitted into care because of their own 'socially unacceptable behaviour' – 2% of admissions between 2005 and 2009 (DCSF, 2009b). The behaviour of some of these children is likely to be problematic because of their experiences with their birth parents, but also because of the disruption and upset associated with having to change where and with whom they live. Finding a care placement often involves children moving schools and thus difficulties in seeing friends, at the same time as children are moved out of their home. In this context, it is not surprising that some children in care can be troublesome and are often troubled, but it is important to emphasise that they are looked after primarily because of what their parents have done, not done, or been able to do, rather than what they – as children – may have done.

It is also important to consider the flaws in 'outcomes' comparisons as a way of evaluating services (Berridge, 2007). A simplistic interpretation may be that these outcomes are due to the care system and that worse outcomes from residential care may mean that residential care is 'worse' than foster care. Usually, managers, politicians, policy makers and academics are not comparing like with like. Comparison is typically made between children in care and the general population, as we have done in Table 2.2. This is fine if the limitations of this sort of presentation are understood, but problematic if they are not. Unthinking use of official data can contribute to the frequently negative views about residential care held by some field social workers and university academics. Certainly, there is evidence of poor practice from those working with children in care, as there is in any profession. However, the realities of managing extremely aggressive or distressed children in care can be overlooked and misunderstood. Cameron and Maginn (2009) describe children entering a residential home in the following way:

> … when children arrived at the children's home, they were mostly unhappy, confused
> and angry, suffering from major attention and concentration difficulties, and exhibiting
> such violent and aggressive behaviour that it was a challenge to get them to settle to
> any activity, let alone more formal lessons in school. (p 5)

These are children who are likely to present a major challenge to most adults and
require a great deal of understanding, patience and skill. Cameron and Maginn (2009)
state that staff are often not trained for the task and yet are left to deal with children
traumatised by their prior experiences in a climate of ill-informed public and official
opinion. They argue that the system holds:

> … carers accountable for the natural but disruptive process of the children working
> through their traumatic pre-care experiences. Ignoring this was like arguing that the
> staff in fracture clinics were somehow responsible for the fact that the clinics are full
> of people with broken limbs! (p 6)

Their conclusion about how to respond to these needs is in the development of a
better trained childcare workforce, one that understands child development and the
effects of the experiences children have had, as well as the knowledge of how to
respond to them. The current system in Britain is a long way off from this ideal. The
RJ approach we research here can be seen as a positive attempt to develop staff skills
in responding to conflict and offending behaviour.

There have been a number of research reviews about 'what works' for children in
care. The most recent (at the time of writing) presents a fairly complex message
and notes that research often reveals serious weaknesses as much as good and
effective practice. Clough and colleagues (2006, pp 86-7) concluded that all studies
at some point tend to stress the importance of listening and responding to young
people's views. The importance of the quality of managers of homes and personal
qualities of care staff is also well evidenced, as is the need for sensitivity to children's
feelings of fear, loss and trauma. They also found considerable evidence of the positive
impact of support, management and training for residential staff in the provision of a
professional service.

Conflict and offending behaviour

So far we have highlighted the well-established associations between a range of
problematic behaviours and poor outcomes in care. Offending behaviour is often
presented as an *outcome* from care, although historically it has often been a *reason* for
care. We noted earlier in this chapter the 19th-century distinctions made between the
'dangerous' and the 'perishing' classes. Several decades ago, the Home Office (1968)
referred to the balance between 'deprivation' and 'depravity' as the cause of criminal
behaviour. A dominant contemporary discourse for both welfare and criminal justice
practitioners is 'risk' or 'risk factors' associated with offending. Rowlands and Statham

(2009) note the acceleration in the use of youth custody during the 1990s, reflecting a hardening of attitudes towards young offenders and leading to a separation of child welfare and youth justice systems. Thus the response to conflict and offending behaviour from children and young people involves an ongoing debate and tension between welfare and justice: help to change versus punishment. As we have seen in Chapter One, this tension is highly pertinent to responding to conflict and offending behaviour through an RJ approach, in that punishing the 'offender' is no longer the focus of the response and the welfare of both 'offender' and 'victim' is of concern. The process aims to change the behaviour of the offender at the same time as providing justice for the victim (and wider community), with reparation being a key part of the RJ process. In this way, the RJ approach represents a way of reconciling the tensions between justice and welfare.

The prevalence of offending in relation to time spent in care can be presented in different ways; government indicators focus on those in care for more than a year. Government 'outcomes' data shows that children in care for one year or more are more likely to have a record of offending than children in the rest of the population – around twice the rate of the general population of children at the time of writing, although the rate was higher in 2001 (three times the rate of the general population). If these data are examined over a longer period, an interesting picture emerges. The overall trend from 2001-07 (see Figure 4.7, Chapter Four) in the general population of children shows an *increase* in the proportion with a record of offending within a year from 3.5% in 2001 to 4.1% in 2007; in comparison, there is a *decrease* in these records for children in care for more than a year from 10.3% in 2001 to 9.5% in 2007. These trends are continuing at the time of writing (the figures for 2008 are 4.3% for all children, 8.8% for children in care) (see for example DCSF, 2009a).

Research often shows a higher prevalence of offending behaviour in correlation with time spent in care. This could be explained by the way research may take longer periods of time as its reference point; for example, it may take into account all instances of an offender's time spent in care. Research on young people in custody and adult prisoners shows that some time in a care background is very common. Hazel and colleagues (2002) found that 41% of children and young people in custody in England and Wales had been in care at some point. On the other hand, Darker and colleagues (2008, p 137) in their analysis of 248 case files of children in care in six different local authorities found that 70% had *no* documented record of offending. The other 30% were made up of those who had offended before entering care (3%), those who did so continuously (before and during care, 17%) and those who only had a record only *after* entry to care (10%). These studies highlight the importance of examining the timing of offending behaviour and the inference we draw from it.

There are a number of ways of explaining the prevalence of offending behaviour and care, although in the main the authors of this volume hold the view that poverty and adverse experiences prior to care are a crucial part of the overall explanation. These adverse experiences can also be seen as a series of 'risk factors' in relation to the development of offending behaviour. Indeed, the policy and practice focus in recent years on 'risk' and 'protective' factors for the development of offending behaviour (see Farrington, 1996; YJB, 2001) has led other researchers to conclude that part of the problem may well be the mix of risk factors concentrated in some care environments (Darker et al, 2008; Marsh, 2008). The potential for the mutual reinforcement of offending behaviour when children are placed together is already well documented (Polsky, 1962; Millham et al, 1975; Sinclair and Gibb, 1998). Adding to this picture, Darker and colleagues (2008) found that offending behaviour was associated with a higher number of placements. This latter evidence means that residential care (often the placement of last resort, following other placement breakdowns) can also be a place that concentrates the risky behaviour that surrounds offending.

Conflict and offending behaviour is more common from children who spend time in residential care than in other types of care placement (Hayden et al, 1999; Taylor, 2003). This pattern is complex and was not confirmed in the quantitative data in the study by Darker et al (2008, p 142). However, Darker and colleagues did find that:

> ... qualitative data from the interviews with young people who had left care suggest that offending behaviour was more common *in certain residential homes* than in other placements. (Emphasis added)

Little (2000, para 7) concludes in his review of a range of Department of Health-commissioned research on children in care that:

Some of society's most damaged young people are placed in residence, including those convicted of grave crimes; and the perpetrators, as well as the victims, of sexual abuse. Typical characteristics staff encounter include chaotic behaviour, fear of going to school; a sense of being lost, having no one and no future; offending; inappropriate sexual behaviour; and difficult relations with parents.

This latter view very much concurs with that of Cameron and Maginn (2009) and highlights the range of complex behaviours that staff encounter and that get young people into (more) trouble when they mix mostly with people like themselves. The Home Office (2004, p 2) recognises that the contraction of residential care has in effect led to a concentration of young people with more challenging behaviours in this environment. However, the factors that predict entry into care are also associated with low educational attainment, which is in turn linked to an increased likelihood of offending behaviour.

So what are we to conclude? The response in most local authorities has been a reduction in residential provision but an ongoing 'crisis' in terms of lack of choice in foster placements and continuing problems with placement breakdown and the associated disruptions for children. Warwickshire closed all local authority children's homes in 1986, although it did so alongside an arrangement with National Children's Homes, the children's charity, for immediate access to four places in a residential home, just over the border from the county. Furthermore, it also used other residential facilities elsewhere, such as residential special schools for children with emotional and behavioural difficulties. The research that evaluated the impact of this policy concluded that there was a major problem with the supply of foster carers, which meant that in most cases there was no possibility of a choice of placement, or of matching a child's needs to the skills and circumstances of the foster carers. The research also concluded that any local authority contemplating a similar move 'should be extremely cautious and consider the negative aspects of such a policy as well as its positives' (Cliffe and Berridge, 1991, p 234). Most subsequent policy in relation to children in care has recognised that residential care is needed for some children, particularly adolescents. Meanwhile the problems with foster carer recruitment and retention, as well as lots of moves of placement for the most problematic (and perhaps unlucky) young people, continue.

From Quality Protects to Care Matters to 'non-negotiable support'

At the time of writing, child welfare services for all children are undergoing far-reaching change, with a view to improving outcomes for *all* children. The Children's Workforce Strategy (DCSF, 2005) sets out to create a more 'joined-up' children's workforce, focused on the needs of children, particularly the most vulnerable. This coincides with developing children's services (which includes education, social care and youth services) as well as children's trusts (which are focused on strengthening accountability and local strategies in respect of children's services). Thus the needs of the most vulnerable or 'at risk' children are part of the work of a service that also provides for those 'in need' and children who use universal or mainstream services. This contemporary focus follows over a decade of initiatives setting out to improve outcomes from education (numerous initiatives and more funding in schools) and combat child poverty and social exclusion (such as Sure Start and the Children's Fund).

There has been a strong focus on children in care in contemporary policy for children and in relation to initiatives to combat social exclusion, particularly since the late 1990s. For example, the Quality Protects programme (DH, 1998) introduced the idea of the 'corporate parent', whereby it was suggested that local councillors should ask themselves whether the services and help for children in care would be good enough for their own children. Funding was provided to local authorities with a focus on improving the 'outcomes' for children in care, with the field of education being a top priority.

A key aspect of attempts to combat social exclusion and improve outcomes from care has been a focus on care leavers. Research in the 1980s established evidence about the vulnerability of young people leaving care (Stein and Carey, 1986), with research in the 1990s updating this evidence (Biehal et al, 1995). The 2000 Children

(Leaving Care) Act arose from a specific government commitment to implement the Utting (1997) *Review of the Safeguards for Children Living Away from Home* and the consultation document *Me Survive Out There* (DH, 1999). The Act came into force in October 2001. Key provisions of the Act include continuing support to young people aged 21 or older, including financial support. A key focus of this support is education and employment, with a clear plan or route to independence (a 'pathway plan') (DCSF, 2009e). Yet Broad's (2005) survey of 52 leaving care teams three years after the implementation of the Act found that:

> ... whilst many services for young people leaving care are improving, the pace of change is very slow, especially in those lower performing and more hard-pressed leaving care teams, where further improvements are largely dependent on external funding. (p 382)

However Broad (2005, p 375) notes a shift in the occupation of young people leaving care, comparing his 2004 survey with his earlier surveys (conducted in 1994 and 1998). In 2004, more young people were in post-16 education and slightly more were in employment; consequently, fewer young people were 'not in employment'. The 2004 survey found that around a third were 'not in employment' (29%) or not working on medical grounds (6%), compared with around half 'not in employment' in 1994 (49%) and 1998 (51.5%). So, while there is evidence of attempts to improve the lot of children leaving care, the overall pace of change is relatively slow, with the gaps between their life chances and those of other children being great and probably widening.

Initiatives aimed at benefiting children generally, such as Every Child Matters (DfES, 2003), children's services and children's trusts, have had their origins in failures in the child protection system. Every Child Matters (ECM) was launched following the Laming enquiry into the death of Victoria Climbié. Once again, children in care were targeted as in need of special help. Arising out of this was the government paper *Choice Protects* (DCSF, 2002), which set out to increase the number of foster placements available for children. Care Matters can be seen as the more specific focus within the ECM framework. Given the number and range of initiatives that have set out to try and improve outcomes for children in care, there is sense of disappointment in the Care Matters White Paper:

> Despite high ambitions and a shared commitment for change, outcomes for children and young people in care have not sufficiently improved. There remains a significant gap between the quality of their lives and those of all children. Tackling this requires urgent action across central and local government, from practitioners in all aspects of children and young people's lives and from their carers, families and friends. (DfES, 2007, p 5)

Care Matters reaffirms the general principle that a family setting is viewed as most beneficial for most children and young people, but that residential care may be more appropriate for some. However, only a quarter of residential homes are reported to meet 90% or more of the government's own national *minimum standards*. The intention is that the inspection system, through compliance notices and the prevention of admission to particular settings, where there are concerns, will be part of the process of driving up standards.

The development of children's departments, within an overall framework of Every Child Matters, means that the education and home environment of children in care fall within the responsibilities of the same department. This means that education and social care staff should be in a better situation for focusing on the needs of the most vulnerable children. As we have outlined in this chapter, there are significant challenges to addressing these needs. There are a number of explanations for the continuing relatively poor circumstances of children leaving the care system. One is the standards agenda that has increased recorded performance generally, particularly in relation to children's educational qualifications; in effect children in care are being compared with a continually improving situation in the general population, but one in which the gap between the most advantaged and most disadvantaged has increased. For example, since 2005, 'all' children's achievement in GCSEs has increased eight percentage points, whereas the achievement of children in care has increased three percentage points (DCSF, 2009a). Another problem, in terms of key issues like educational achievement and employment, is the well-documented and relative inequality in British society. A recent evaluation of attempts to reduce poverty and inequality since 1997 shows a complex picture, with Britain still being one of the most unequal societies in Europe (Hills et al, 2009). Relative poverty matters in relation to the situation of children in care because they are more likely to come from poor families with the well-known associated disadvantages in all sorts of life chances and opportunities.

The Youth Crime Action Plan, launched in 2008, interrelates with the key objectives of Every Child Matters (see also Chapter One). Pertinent to the focus of the current chapter is the extension of intensive fostering schemes as an alternative to custody (HM Government, 2009). Targeted youth support (TYS) is another cross-departmental, multidisciplinary concept that includes a range of agencies working on a diversity of problems, as encapsulated in the following quote:

> Led by Children's Trusts, working closely with partners such as Connexions, schools, health services and voluntary and community agencies, the TYS multi-agency, early intervention and prevention approach tackles the root causes of poor outcomes such as teenage pregnancy, substance misuse and youth offending, all key aims of the youth public service agreement (PSA) target which focuses on increasing the numbers of young people on the path to success. (DCSF, 2009e, para 3)

The language of 'non-negotiable support' can also be seen as indicative of the sense of frustration evident in other government documents and some commentary in relation to youth crime and social exclusion, as well as in Care Matters (as highlighted above). This frustration arises from a sense that successive governments that have explicitly focused on these issues since 1997 have failed to get to the most vulnerable, some of whom are children in residential care.

Cameron and Maginn (2009) conclude that given the amount of targeted funding for children in care in Britain in recent years, it would seem unlikely that the obvious failings can be ascribed largely to resources or political apathy. They point out that there is a large workforce of around 170,000 adults responsible for around 60,000 children at any one time and that perhaps we need to look more closely at how people are trained and what it is they are doing (and are asked to do) within their work role. One of the issues for these authors is the move away from the 'parenting' role in the care system towards that of 'carer'. They note the important, but subtle, difference between being cared for (for example, by a babysitter or childminder) and being parented, with all the complex and long-term responsibilities this entails.

An additional issue that is important to the quality of care children experience within the care system is whether the professionals responsible for them are appropriately trained and supported. Gupta and Blewett (2007) highlight the evidence about both the quantity and quality of people working with children. They conclude that the implications of these deficits are so serious that failure to analyse and address them will undermine the ambitions of the Children's Workforce Strategy. Specifically, they refer to the 'crisis' in childcare social work as particularly acute. The 'crisis' is deepening at the time of writing, following the aftermath of the Baby P case that came to the attention of the public in 2008. Even prior to this very high-profile and critical case, Gupta and Blewett (2007) report 'a universal belief in the dominant image of social work being a negative one ... contributing to low morale and to a sense of not being valued' (p 174).

In conclusion, this chapter has painted a picture of a service under pressure. In particular, residential care is reluctantly accepted as needed, but often misunderstood. Further, the children and young people in residential care are often those who are the most vulnerable and disrupted, whose behaviour is difficult to manage. The next chapter will take a closer look at residential care in our case study local authority.

3

Background to the research

Introduction

This chapter describes the situation in residential care in the case study local authority at the time of the field research, reflecting on the changes observed since research was undertaken in the same local authority in the mid-1990s. Comments made by care staff during the course of the current field research are included in this account, as is documentary evidence and observation. Other research has tracked the changes in the residential care environment by revisiting children's care homes (see Berridge and Brodie, 1998). This can be a useful way of identifying how policy and practice influences the everyday living environment of children in residential care. Having explained the nature and context of children's residential care in this local authority; the chapter goes on to outline the approach taken in the research and the range of data collected in the research.

Residential care in the case study local authority

The case study local authority is a large county authority with a wide range of social circumstances, including large areas of social housing and forces accommodation, as well as leafy suburbs and affluent areas. At the time of the field research, the total population in care over a year was over 1,000 children, of whom less than 60 were in residential care (for children without disabilities) at any one time in local authority homes, although over 100 were resident over a year (near to the national average for the proportion of children in residential care at the time of the research). The population of this local authority is overwhelmingly White British (93%), so any comparison by ethnicity in this study is limited. For example, one of the 16 case studies reported in Chapter Seven raises some very specific issues. Also, the implementation of a restorative justice (RJ) approach focused wholly on children *without* disabilities. The local authority is similar in many key outcomes indicators to counties in the same area of England and is generally around the national average in terms of the rate of offending recorded among children in care.

At the time of the field research, the local authority had an established residential care strategy based on a split between short-term and long-term homes. Five of the ten homes in the research were locally based, short-term homes. 'Short-term' was defined as a stay of 'up to six months'. The emphasis in these short-term homes was on shared care wherever possible, with increasing contact with parents. The four long-term homes were viewed as a county resource and had a therapeutic emphasis. The original residential care strategy was based on the desire to keep children with significant and complex needs within the local authority, rather than move them to an 'out of county' placement. Nine of the ten homes were open facilities with an average of six beds. One of the short-term units also had an emergency bed, where young people usually stayed only one night (during the week) and perhaps two or three nights if they were admitted at the weekend. The remaining home was bigger and designated as a secure unit (a locally based secure children's home); this was both a county and regional resource that catered for a few welfare cases, as well as children detained by the courts. The dynamic and changing environment of residential care was apparent even by the second year of the research (2007), when two of the open and short-term homes in the study were closed – one permanently and (pertinent to the focus of the current research) one for refurbishment – following significant difficulties managing young people's behaviour.

Children's homes are highly regulated environments; this meant that all kinds of documented evidence were available to the researchers about the situation prior to our fieldwork. Echoing concerns about the quality of care at the national level (already noted in Chapter Two in relation to the Care Matters initiative), there was evidence from inspections in our local authority on the lack of progress in some of the national standards set. The inspection system can be seen as an interesting device for blame shifting, in that many of the issues noted related to the availability of resources, rather than practice issues.

An internal review of the safety of children's homes conducted just prior to the start of the current research also provided evidence about a number of positive, as well as problematic, aspects of the sector in the case study local authority. In this review, the managers of residential units were said to be well qualified and working in a climate of mutual respect with senior managers in the local authority. Furthermore, they were said to be well supported by the local authority. Statements of purpose of homes were reported to be 'generally clear' and homes were described as 'generally safe places to live'. The report concluded that there was evidence of structured environments that supported young people. Furthermore, the relationship between inspectors and managers was described as 'mature and mostly positive, providing opportunities for constructive discussion'. The handling and recording of critical incidents was said to be 'largely sound'. It was noted that the department had invested heavily in staff training to avoid the use of physical restraint, namely the 'Team-Teach' approach (see Team-Teach, 2003) as well as staff training in 'restorative justice' techniques (that is, the focus of the current study). The internal review concluded that these whole-service training programmes had resulted in a 'laudable consistency of approach to young people with limited use of recorded physical restraints'.

Concern in the review focused mainly on the physical environment and infrastructure of homes, as well as certain systems in operation. For example, some of the buildings were said to be 'below par' and in relation to periods awaiting repairs being undertaken, the review warned that the local authority 'runs the risk of an embarrassing prosecution' if the recommendations of inspections are not carried out.

Although policies and procedures affecting safety were generally consistently applied, improved internal monitoring was said to be needed. Improvements in homes were noted since the earlier inspection report, with one exception. It was said that the inspectors were rightly concerned about requirements and recommendations ignored 'even if it is the system that has militated against them'. Alternative ways of handling emergency placements were said to be needed due to a minority of managers being directed to take young people.

A consultation involving six young people (from three different homes) was held as part of this review. This consultation raised some important issues that were used to inform the interviews and questionnaires with young people reported in the research in this volume. Issues raised by young people in the internal review related to the use of punishments and 'sanctions', which were sometimes seen as too harsh; fairness and consistency from staff; and the view that their complaints and concerns should be taken seriously. Young people also raised broader issues about wanting to be able to lead a life like most other teenagers. These included having their friends to visit and being allowed more freedom and independence as they got older, as well as specific issues such as having a lock on their bedroom door, with their own key.

Observations on the changing residential care setting

The researchers made careful observations of the setting in which residential care was operating and the changes apparent. Observations of change were possible because earlier research had been carried out in the same local authority as part of a bigger project involving other local authorities (see Hayden and Gorin, 1998). Key overall changes included the reduction in the number of residential care units in the case study local authority over a 10-year period, from 17 in 1996 to 10 in 2006 at the start of the research; a reduction in the average number of children in homes, from eight in 1996 to six in 2006, and consequently an improved staffing ratio; and a clearer remit (or 'statement of purpose') for individual units. Other changes observed (and sometimes commented on by staff) during the course of fieldwork are discussed in the following account.

Externally, most of the homes looked fairly well kept in terms of paintwork and in comparison with neighbouring properties, and some managed to maintain a homely feel to them. They were better than one could have been led to expect from the internal review document referred to above. The purpose of most homes was not immediately obvious to the casual observer. Often the only indication that a home might not be occupied by a family was the number of cars parked outside it on a day when a staff meeting was taking place, or the presence of a mini-bus. Several managers mentioned that at some point a neighbour had been surprised to learn that the building was a children's home. On the other hand, in a couple of locations, the home had become notorious and problems reported by neighbours threatened the future of the home. Indeed, one of the home closures already referred to during the period of research was due to an ongoing campaign from local residents. A similar closure of a home occurred during the earlier (1996) period of research.

Reflecting the comments noted earlier from inspectors, it was obvious that many care staff and managers were very experienced: overall, around 45% of care staff had 10 or more years' experience of working in residential care. Five of the ten managers had worked in the residential sector for more than 20 years. A strong sense of camaraderie was evident in several of the fieldwork visits – it was clear that despite some differences of opinion, staff did generally get on well with each other and staff meetings were important events for bringing people together. It was obvious that staff felt able to disagree in public and in all homes the managers were happy to allow us to have time with staff groups, as well as young people, without them being present.

Types of care environment

Fieldwork quickly illustrated that the differences between long-term and short-term homes were not always evident because of the pressures to place young people or because a short-term placement did not end as planned. In particular, the split between 'long-term' and 'short-term' homes did not always seem so obvious in relation to the homes for older adolescents. For example, one young person told us how she had been living in a 'short-term' home for around a year and saw this placement as where she lived. Yet she had to share her home with a continuing stream of 'emergency' placements that stayed one or two days.

The reality of managing residential care as a scarce resource meant that there was rarely any choice of placement or any real ability for staff to consider the impact of a particular admission on the whole group. This situation particularly related to the homes for teenagers. The situation is summarised in the following quote:

> 'The ideal scenario would be to look at the mix ... the reality is a phone call. If there's a spare bed, it's the next available person.'

Interviews with some of the young people (reported in Chapter Six) reflected the situation portrayed in the last quote, particularly in the short-term home with the emergency bed, where many of those admitted were young people in crisis. In this home, staff described young people as 'hard to place' and the home was described as 'the end of the line' in the local authority (before secure accommodation); the reality was said to be that young people went in and out of foster care placements and back to this home:

> 'Many come backwards and forwards. All want to stay.'

Two of the four long-term homes accommodated younger children in the county who were usually aged between nine and 13 years. These homes were able to stick more clearly to their remit and plan admissions. These homes for younger children had a more positive feel to them and reported good relationships with neighbours too. As one of the managers said, "many of the children can be very charming" to neighbours and so on, because they wanted to be liked. Almost all the children were in full-time education and schools were described as supportive.

A key difference between the open homes and secure home was taken up at interviews conducted with staff in the secure home. Staff in this home saw young people as 'a captive audience' where it became both more essential to address conflict and easier to find the right time to do this, because the young people weren't 'going anywhere'. More generally, it was obvious that a tightly structured day, the provision of education on site and the related expectation that young people got up and went to the education area, as well as good sports and other facilities, made for a very ordered and purposeful atmosphere. One of the young people interviewed in this secure unit reported how the restrictions meant:

'I'm getting healthy, they don't let you smoke or drink and you have to be in your room at 9.30 [pm].'

Another young person said:

'I'm back in education here. I'd forgotten how much I liked school.'

Nine of the 10 homes accommodated both boys and girls; with one home specialising in working with teenage girls. The 10 children's homes were therefore varied types of places; they were also located in different types of area and were very widely distributed geographically across the whole county. Three were in predominantly urban areas, several were on the suburban or semi-rural fringe of bigger settlements and some were in areas of expensive, large, detached, older housing. There were long distances between some homes, an issue of great significance when a young person was moved from short-stay to long-stay accommodation. The practicality of a young person staying in regular contact with friends or continuing to go to their school or educational facility could be an issue. For example, a young woman (aged 16) interviewed during the course of the research described how (officially) she could only see her boyfriend about once a week, because he lived over 20 miles away and she had only one train pass a week. This young woman was frequently reported missing when she left the home for periods to be with this young man. Another issue was the relatively affluent and suburban environment in which some homes were situated; this could mean that local schools were sought after and not always perceived by care staff as sympathetic to the needs of children in care.

Education

Chapter Two (Table 2.2) highlights the big disparity between the educational achievements of children in care and those of all children. This monitoring data also show that children in care are much more likely to have a statement for special educational need, be excluded from school or miss school through non-attendance (DCSF, 2009a). Local authorities are legally required to promote the educational achievement of children in care under section 52 of the 2004 Children Act. This legal requirement follows a long history of documented concerns about the access to education and achievement of children in care (see, for example, Jackson, 1989). Thus the pressure is on for residential homes to make improvements in how they facilitate and encourage access to education and achievement. Overall, in most homes there was a general sense that access to education and schooling was taken seriously and the education inclusion team was well regarded. This team provided targeted support to children in care that could include a couple of hours of individual support and troubleshooting for children off school, as well as support for care staff and social workers in relation to understanding and getting the best out of the education system for these children. Yet overall, educational provision was very varied across the county, as were the needs of the children, with access to full-time mainstream education being more typical of the younger children.

Compared with 1996, the availability of space designated for educational purposes and for the use of computers was striking and evident in every home. In the two homes for younger children, fieldwork visits illustrated that these facilities were used if children were at home during the school day. One of these homes had a special session one evening a week in which a computer 'expert' came in to develop activities on computers with staff and children. It was clear, however, that staff confidence in supporting children with their education was very variable and this was often reflected in their attitude towards the role of computers in supporting education. For some staff, there was a tendency to focus on the idea that the internet was potentially an avenue for access to inappropriate material or predatory adults as a reason for restricting access to the internet. In some homes, there was even ambivalence towards having an 'education room'; indeed, staff sometimes avoided calling the room the education room. Often staff in open homes wanted to make it clear that they were not teachers and in terms of educational provision wanted to see children going to school:

> 'Home is not an alternative to school so we try and make it as boring as possible and encourage them to get back to school and meet their friends and all the positive things about school.'

The latter comment reflects the view in many open homes that there was tension between educational provision within the home to relieve boredom and the potential impact of that provision on a young person's desire to go to school. The expectation that young people would at least do school work in the education room during the morning was evident not only by what was said, but also by what was witnessed during visits to homes. Yet the reality of access to mainstream education meant that in two of the homes for teenagers (one short-term, one long-term) in more affluent semi-rural/suburban locations it was "rare to have a young person in mainstream school". In both homes, the local secondary school was popular and oversubscribed. Furthermore, as one of the managers said, "Frankly our young people don't feel comfortable there anyway." The other manager said, "It always feels that people are being critical of us because we've got people off school." Yet this manager said that they thought that sometimes provision of only a few afternoons a week was realistic, given a young person's state of mind, ability to concentrate and general behaviour in a group setting. Distance from home and original school was a factor in certain short-term units, as the young people could come from anywhere in the county. Nevertheless, the manager did see major improvements in their working with the local pupil referral unit and the home could access this provision more easily.

In some homes (most obviously those with younger children), individuals from the county education inclusion team for children in care provided very effective and well-appreciated support:

> 'Amazing, she gets kids into school, provides support in school, sorts out problems, advises the home on education. She tries to come to the staff meetings when we talk about kids....'

Overall, some managers perceived 'changes for the better' in the way the education service (and county team for children in care) supported and provided for children.

In relation to special schools, the manager of one of the homes for younger children said:

> 'On the whole we have a very good relationship ... there have been some issues about us removing children from school. We will not come in and remove them from school. We'll come up to the gate.... We're not going in to remove them.... It gives our children the wrong message about us ... that we'll come in whatever. Whilst they are in school it is their responsibility....'

And, in mainstream schools:

> 'We've got some really good relationships. We had one child who hadn't been in school for two years and [staff] got them into a really good school. You couldn't get a more caring staff..... One [young person] is like living with Tigger but the school is very good with him.'

In both of the homes for younger children, all but one of the residents was in full-time schooling. In one of these homes, a child was given a fixed period of exclusion after he "badly assaulted a teacher". In the other home, a child was being educated within the home because he had absconded from school shortly after admission and had gone missing for a week, leading to a police search for him (he had been hidden within his family who lived near the school).

However, in one area of the county, facilities for children outside mainstream education and special schools had been concentrated on one site. For young people of secondary school age, this was seen as 'disastrous'. The response to behaviour problems was said generally to be to reduce educational contact time, so that all young people in this home had only part-time educational provision or they did not attend. This situation tended to increase the pressures on staff and conflict within homes.

In contrast, all the young people in secure accommodation had a very full and structured day, both in education and in the other activities available on site, as noted earlier. Furthermore, all care staff were expected to spend time supporting young people within their teaching groups, so that the connection between care and education was enhanced. However, this latter situation was not popular with all care staff, partly because of their own worries about having the relevant knowledge and expertise to support young people with their education.

Health and wellbeing

As with issues concerning education, the negative differences in health and wellbeing evident among children in care compared with children in the general population are well documented (see, for example, Wyler, 2000). Higher rates of substance misuse, teenage pregnancy and mental health problems interrelate with other forms of disadvantage, making children in care vulnerable to getting into more trouble and impeding access to positive activities that can enhance their future life chances. Some of these issues also relate to the problem behaviour presented, particularly in the residential context. Department of Health guidance (DH, 2002) has been around for some time and the Care Matters agenda (DfES, 2007) makes this guidance statutory.

In our case study local authority, access to dedicated psychological and therapeutic support usually meant a long wait for access to mainstream child and adolescent mental health services in 1996. By 2006, support was improving, with plans for all homes to have their own part-time therapist. In practice, this had not happened successfully in some of the units visited, either because of therapists leaving or because of problems with recruitment (which was said to be because of the low salary offered). As has been noted in relation to access to schools and educational support, the homes for younger children tended to be better served than homes for teenagers. For example, one of the homes for younger children had a half-time art and drama therapist. Every child in the home had a session with her every week, unless they already arrived with some form of therapy in place. This therapist had a well-equipped room that opened on to a 'therapeutic garden', with a seat, water feature, plants and so on. She also ran group sessions, such as sexuality awareness, as and when the need arose.

In the other home for younger children, the therapist came to all staff meetings. The first hour of the meeting was taken up with key workers talking about their children and the therapist responding with ideas and strategies. She also had a drop-in session for the children. This therapist undertook individual work, depending on whether the children had existing support on arrival at the home. At the time of a fieldwork visit, staff said, "We find her invaluable." Some homes also had support from educational psychologists (EPs). In one case, the individual did lots of work with the home for a couple of terms before leaving the post: "She was seen as excellent. She interacted well with the staff." Overall, however, there were problems recruiting suitable individuals to some of the therapeutic posts and the support from EPs varied and to some extent depended on the special interests of the individuals involved. Furthermore, it appeared that the style of therapy offered was very much a matter of the therapists' preferences, rather than the needs identified by a particular children's home. On the other hand, the presence of this kind of support did help the more receptive staff develop a better understanding of children's behaviour.

Behaviour management

Staff perceptions were of an increasingly difficult client group. Nevertheless, there was an evident shift in philosophy and practice, away from controlling techniques and physical intervention towards de-escalation and conflict resolution wherever possible. At the time of the earlier research (Hayden and Gorin, 1998), children's residential care staff were trained by hospital psychiatric staff in the use of physical restraint, using the now discredited 'control and restraint' method. Following this research, there was a move away from the latter method, with whole-staff training in the Team-Teach approach (Team-Teach, 2003), which emphasises de-escalation techniques and the use of 'positive handling strategies' only in the most extreme circumstances. Therefore, although behaviour management issues continued to be an ongoing issue for staff, practice was already changing before the RJ training took place.

There was stronger evidence of security measures than would have been usual 10 years ago. For example, in certain homes, education rooms and lounges were locked unless young people asked for access and were supervised. In two homes, staff appeared to spend considerable amounts of time behind the locked door of the staff office. The language of a prison or correctional environment was in evidence during one interview with the manager of an open home, where the term 'lock-down' was used to describe the response to the handling of a serious incident.

Nevertheless, physical intervention (or restraint) was not common (corroborating the evidence from the internal review referred to earlier in this chapter). Where there was physical contact it appeared that this was recorded on the incident records reported on in Chapter Seven. For example, one senior member of care staff, despite describing very difficult to manage behaviour, saw some improvements compared with the previous year, such as a reduction in physical interventions, referred to as 'restraint', which "used to be daily a year ago". Changes in practice in relation to resolving conflict, following the RJ training, had meant that "now we try not to intervene ... only if a young person is harming somebody". Ongoing training in the already established 'Team-Teach' approach to managing behaviour was also credited for discouraging the use of restraint, as this approach was said to encourage staff not to use restraint (referred to as 'positive handling strategies') "unless it is absolutely necessary".

What is the future for children's residential care?

We noted in Chapter Two that residential care has suffered from a 'last resort' status for some time now and that the aftermath of enquiries into abusive regimes has not helped the image of, and morale in, the service. In Campbell's (2009) view:

> For the last forty years – or maybe more – there has been a substantial number of field social workers who have been implacably opposed to residential child care. Many of them have moved into managerial or lecturing jobs, and they have taken their opinions with them, influencing the policies of the agencies they work in and the tone of the training of the next generation of social workers. (para 1)

Although current policy acknowledges the need for residential care, the general message is that although this may be necessary, it is not desirable. In this context, it is hard for some staff to feel that they are trusted, respected and valued. As one member of staff remarked during the course of the research, "I don't tell people exactly what I do". This person felt that there were all sorts of negative associations attached to residential childcare. Despite this, some of the changes noted above, such as the increased emphasis on education and therapeutic support, are clearly positive. The interest of staff in trying to develop new ways of managing difficult behaviour is also a positive indicator of a service that is still evolving and trying to improve the quality of care provided.

Introducing a restorative justice approach to children's residential care

The decision to introduce an RJ approach into residential care in this local authority was made in 2004. Training of all staff was undertaken during 2005 and early 2006. The training involved a three-day course and was mandatory. This initial training focused on scripted conferences where the 'encounter' for all involved is at its most formal (on the RJ continuum, see Figure 1.1 in Chapter One). It was emphasised that the script could be adapted to particular circumstances. The 'script' put forward the order and method of questioning in a conference. Refresher training was carried out one year later and focused more on the informal or everyday use of RJ as a style of communication, with the 'encounter' aspect being more everyday and low key.

Although rates of offending for children in care had been going up in the local authority at the time that the RJ approach was planned and agreed, addressing rates of offending was not the only motivating factor. Other issues documented in internal reports noted that 'anti-social behaviour' and 'disruptive behaviour' as well as staff relationship and workplace issues might be addressed by introducing RJ. Furthermore, the broader aims of improving the working environment of staff and the living environment of children were seen to be of crucial importance.

Nevertheless, local authority documentation revealed that reducing police call-outs and offending levels for looked after children were the key *official* reasons for introducing an RJ approach. Offending rates are an outcome indicator for children looked after for more than a year; Performance and Assessment Framework (PAF) C18 relates to the percentage of children aged 10 years and over (and who are looked after for at least 12 months) given a final warning, reprimand or conviction in a year (see Table 2.2 in Chapter Two for national data and Figures 4.6 and 4.7 in Chapter Four for trend data on offending and children in care in the case study local authority). It was known at the start of the research that the *number of individual children* who have a record of offending is small; therefore, the percentage change in this indicator is effected by a handful of children (and very particular and individual circumstances). The focus in the performance indicator was based on between 34 and 59 individual children (depending on the year; see Figure 4.6, Chapter Four) of the 500 or so children who have been in care for more than a year, from a total population of looked after children of more than 1,000 in the local authority. Further analysis of data for a one-year period showed that across the whole population of children in care (the 1,000-plus children in care, including those in care for less than one year as well as those who are included in the performance indicator), only 84 individual children had a record of offending, for whom 114 offences were recorded. Of the 84 individuals, 39 had been looked after for 12 months or more (and were therefore the focus of the PAF C18 indicator). Around half of the individuals (18 of the 39) were in residential care, with most of these being in local authority homes.

Contact with care staff from homes prior to starting the field research revealed that some were uncomfortable with the criminal justice language of 'victim' and 'offender' and indeed with the concept of restorative *justice*. However, the local authority used the term restorative justice in its promotional literature and clearly saw the adoption of the process as something they were trying to do with other agencies, such as the youth offending team (YOT). The local authority emphasised from the outset that implementing RJ was not seen as a 'quick fix':

This is a long-term programme of culture change, which will involve all of our staff in children's residential homes, managers and other partners such as police, health workers and teachers. (Local authority promotional material, 2005)

The local authority promotional literature clearly explained the key restorative concepts of 'responsibility, reparation and reintegration'. The training literature used both restorative *justice* and restorative *approaches* in relation to what the local authority was doing, with an emphasis very much on the more formal use in meetings and conferences.

Research methodology

Timescale and approach

The field research was undertaken in two phases, the first in autumn 2006 and the second in autumn 2007, with organisational data being analysed over a longer period. The overall research design is best described as an evaluation, involving the collection and triangulation of a range of types of data before, during and after the implementation of an RJ approach across all children's residential units in one local authority. In a sense, this provided the opportunity for a natural experiment in which any change could be tracked over both an extended time period (2001-07) as well as a more focused one (2006 and 2007), with the latter time period being after all care staff had been trained in the same RJ approach. Like most natural experiments conducted in a service setting, this study presented lots of complexity and potential for multiple influences and measures of 'success' or 'failure'. For this reason, we were influenced by the way a realist evaluation recognises the complexity of 'real world' settings and avoids the use of single measures of effectiveness:

Realism does not rely on a single outcome measure to deliver a pass/fail verdict on a programme.... A key requirement of realist evaluation is thus to take heed of the different layers of social reality which make up and surround programmes. (Pawson and Tilley, 2004, p 8)

Further:

Realist evaluations asks not, 'What works?' or, 'Does this program work?' but asks instead, 'What works for whom in what circumstances and in what respects, and how?' (Pawson and Tilley, 2004, p 2)

Although our study does not meet the full criteria for a realist evaluation, we have borrowed concepts from this approach because it helps make sense of the complexity of the research setting and data collected. It also helps situate the implementation of the RJ approach in children's residential care. Pawson and Tilley (2004) argue that programmes or interventions (in the current research, RJ) are based on a vision or theory of change. The theory underpinning the use of RJ as a programme to address conflict and offending behaviour in children's residential care might be explained as operating in the following context-mechanism-outcomes configuration.

Contexts (those features of the conditions in which programmes are introduced that are relevant to the operation of the programme mechanisms)

Different types of children's residential care homes (secure, open, long-stay, short-stay, younger children aged nine to 13, teenagers aged 13 and over) as places where conflict and offending behaviour might occur or emanate. Staff all have the requisite training, but will have different attitudes towards, and experiences and understandings of, young people's behaviour. Attitudes, experiences and understandings of agencies external to residential care will also vary (for example, police, YOT, schools).

Mechanisms (what it is about programmes or interventions that is likely to bring about an effect)

Young people, through the actions and responses of staff trained in the use of an RJ approach, will develop more empathy for others, learn to resolve conflict and address offending behaviour through the RJ encounter and process. They will learn to take responsibility and make amends for wrongdoing through the process of reparation. Staff in turn will have a way of resolving more conflicts without resorting to external help, particularly the police.

Desired outcomes (what the adoption of an RJ approach is trying to achieve)

Reductions in conflict and offending behaviour; residential homes become a better place to live and work.

Our study does not meet the more exacting criteria for a full realist evaluation in that in essence it is a simple before and after design (Tilley, 2009); we do not have comparison groups and the number of children in different types of residential care within one local authority is far too small to allow the creation of comparison groups about which we could calculate a differential effect from the use of an RJ approach. Nevertheless, what we lack in these respects we believe we compensate for in depth and range of data and thereby add to what is known about implementing an RJ approach in a particular context.

We see our research on this local authority as a case study in which a whole-service approach to behaviour management was being implemented (the RJ approach). The research tracks both processes and outcomes from training all residential care staff in this approach. The training was completed in the year before the research fieldwork started, so that at the time of the first phase of fieldwork (autumn 2006) it was between six months and a year (depending on the timing of training) since the initial training. By the time of the second phase of fieldwork (autumn 2007), refresher training had also taken place (for home managers and lead coordinators for RJ). Throughout the period of the research, workshops were held with registered managers and RJ coordinators. In addition, a steering group met a number of times; this group included senior managers from across children's services, a children's home registered manager and a range of people from other organisations, such as the police, the Children's Fund and the YOT. The research tracks any changes over time, both from secondary data available from within the local authority, as well as through fieldwork. The key changes that were investigated in the fieldwork were staff attitudes towards the use of RJ and the way in which it was being used. Other parts of the research used existing organisational data (from 2001 to 2007) to track any evidence of changes in resolving conflict that may relate to how RJ is being used, both across the service (for example, by looking at the pattern of police call-outs and incident reports) and in relation to individual children (by conducting a cohort study as well as individual case studies).

The design of the research was agreed by negotiation with key members of the local authority and after an initial review of the literature on RJ. Researchers also attended the local authority steering group and RJ workshops. Attendance at these events added to the researchers' understanding and insight into how the RJ approach was likely to work in different types of residential home; it also afforded access to key staff that helped pave the way for fieldwork. For example, care staff helped in piloting and refining research instruments used and as key contacts in the units visited as part of the research. In addition, residential staff were trained and involved in collecting the data in the case studies of individual children. Local authority staff were also involved in collecting data in the cohort study and the police collated data on police call-outs.

Aim

The research aimed to evaluate the impact of a restorative justice approach on the working and living environment of [name of local authority] children's residential care, specifically in relation to conflict resolution and offending behaviour.

Objectives

The objectives of the research were as follows:

- to establish the extent to which an RJ approach is being used in children's residential care and how it is being used, from the perspective of managers, home staff and young people;

- to investigate any changes in perception of the use of an RJ approach and its impact on the working and living environment over a one-year period, from the perspective of managers, home staff and young people;
- to track any changes in offending, police call-outs and other relevant issues;
- to track outcomes, over a year, for a cohort of young people, resident or admitted to the 10 units in a one-month period;
- to conduct case studies of individual young people focusing on the nature of and responses to problematic behaviour and the overall assessment of the impact of the current care episode.

Research ethics

As with all social research conducted for a local authority, the research design had to be submitted for scrutiny by research governance procedures. It was also submitted to the relevant faculty research ethics committee at the University of Portsmouth. The main issues raised by this scrutiny related to informed consent and the specific considerations of conducting research with children, specifically children in the care of the local authority. Both field researchers had Criminal Records Bureau checks. There was some debate between the local authority, the researchers and the university ethics committee about parental consent and young people's consent in research. Of note is the stance of the local authority representatives who were keen that children had their own individual right to be asked whether they participated (or not) in the research, whereas it is usual in social research that parents are asked before their children are approached and asked whether they want to participate. Children in care are not always in a directly comparable situation to other children. The local authority has parental responsibility for some children (for example, those on full care orders) and in this case the local authority was also the commissioner of the research and wanted to obtain the views of young people. In other cases, where parental responsibility was shared, relationships were not always straightforward, either between the parents and the local authority, or between the parents and children (or indeed both). We resolved the situation with the help of the Barnardo's guidelines on researching children. These guidelines include advice about asking children to participate in research where parental responsibility and contact may be problematic (see Barnardo's, 2006). We discuss researching children in more detail in Chapter Six.

We agreed that all social workers, parents and care staff in contact with children resident in the homes during the period of field research should be made aware of the plans to include children's views in the research. Social workers were made aware so that they knew what was planned and could deal with any queries from parents and so that they could raise any concerns about approaching a particular child. Parents were sent letters from the individual residential home, informing them about the research and including a response slip if they wanted to 'opt out' of the research on behalf of their child; two parents did so. The units were sent copies of the questionnaires and an information sheet for the young people in advance of the visit. By the time the researchers visited the homes, many of the young people were clearly well prepared by the staff and knew broadly what the research was about. Young people themselves were approached at the time of the visit and asked whether they were willing to take part in the research. Some were initially a little wary and there were five outright refusals. Often, however, young people did want to have their say once they saw other young people doing so. Children in some homes in the first round of field research were willing to talk, but did not want to complete the research questionnaires. After interviews were completed with the young people available and willing to take part in the research, the participants were thanked and told that the home was to be given a £20 HMV voucher as a 'thank you' for their participation. Some homes wanted the voucher to be given directly to the young person; others wanted it to be left with staff.

It should be noted that absolute confidentiality cannot be given when researching children in matters relating to their safety and that of others. Children were made aware of this at the start of any contact and no questions were designed to elicit this sort of data. This information was also made available in writing in the 'Information to young people'. Ahead of conducting the field research, named individuals within the local authority children's department were made available as the first point of contact for researchers who were concerned by what children told them during the course of the research.

Key aspects of the research

At the time of agreeing the research design, it was made clear that all data would be treated as confidential (noting, of course, the limits to this in the context of research involving children) and made anonymous in the course of analysis. Great care was taken in explaining this to staff at the start of fieldwork interviews. All managers had their interviews recorded and a transcript was sent back to them for amendment or comment about any quotes or other information they did not want to appear in the report of the research. The manager of the secure unit in the local authority was offered the additional assurance (because they were identifiable) that they would be given sight of a draft if an identifiable quote might be used in the final report, so that if they had any concerns they could ask for it to be removed or reworded. Staff group interviews were not recorded after the first two staff groups indicated that they were not happy with this. Interviews with young people were not recorded. With staff groups and young people, notes were made during and after interviews and both groups provided written comments within their questionnaire responses.

In conclusion, this chapter has set out to give some sense of the challenges posed in trying to effect positive organisational change in children's residential care. Residential care is an important, but residual, provision for some of the most damaged children in society and as such it provides a real test bed for an intervention that aims to provide a different way of responding to conflict and addressing the needs of 'victims' and 'offenders'.

Table 3.1: Overview of data collected in the research

Data types and sources	Quantity and timescale		Purpose/focus
Care staff and managers	*2006*	*2007*	Staff perceptions and
Questionnaires	103	3	experiences; actual use
Group interviews (care staff)	11	9	of RJ
Individual interviews (managers)	10	9	Whether any change
			Comparison – managers
			and care staff
Children	*2006*	*2007*	Children's perceptions of
Questionnaires	21	17	behaviour management
Interviews	26	17	in residential care
			Whether they understood
			the RJ concept
Context and process			How homes were run,
Observations – homes and	Made during visits to		interaction between
interaction	homes 2006 and 2007		staff and young people.
			Residential environment,
Observations – organisational and	Ongoing autumn 2006–		etc
implementation issues (steering	June 2008		
group, RJ groups and interim			Helped develop our
reports to RJ coordinators and			research questions;
managers)			verify/test our
			observations and findings
'Outcomes' for children			
Cohort study	46 children, 12 months		Particular focus on
	2006-07		offending and known risk
			factors
Case studies	16 children, summer		Investigated behaviour and
	2007		its management, impact
			of care at an individual
			level
			Whether RJ evidenced
Organisational change: outcome indicators			
Police call-outs	2001-07		Whether key
Incident records	2001-07		organisational data
Records of offending	2001-07		demonstrated change
Out-of-hours service	2006 and 2007		

Problem and offending behaviours in residential care

4

Introduction

This chapter focuses on the various forms of evidence about the nature, prevalence and trends in problem and offending behaviours in the 10 children's homes in the study. The sources of data in this chapter are based on four sets of organisational records: incident records from care staff (2001-07); police call-outs to homes (2001-07); number and proportion of children looked after for more than a year with a record of offending (2001-07); and use of the out-of-hours service in two comparable periods during the field research (2006 and 2007). When interpreting this trend data, the reader is reminded that all staff were trained in the use of a restorative justice (RJ) approach during 2005, with some staff completing the course in early 2006. In addition, evidence from staff interviews (reported in depth in Chapter Five in relation to implementing RJ) is cited in this chapter where this helps to illustrate issues relating to managing problem and offending behaviours in residential care.

Living in residential care

Care and 'risk'

It has already been noted in Chapter Two that problem and offending behaviours have long been associated with the care experience, particularly in relation to the residential care environment. This has helped to further stigmatise young people in care, with some debate about the extent to which the residential care environment may itself be 'criminogenic', inferring that the environment or context of care adds to the risks of becoming involved in crime. It is a concept based on the risk and protective factors paradigm that offers one explanation of the development of offending behaviour (see, for example, Farrington, 1996). We know that children in care have more risks in their lives than most children in the community. We also know that the likelihood of offending increases when more risks are present and that life-course transitions and turning points are very important in relation to the development of anti-social and offending behaviour (Farrington, 2002).

So what is it about being in residential care that might add to or amplify the existing risks that a young person *in residential care* gets involved in problem or offending behaviour? At the very least, going into care represents a turning point in a young person's life and one that may prove positive or negative. We have already highlighted in Chapters Two and Three that residential care, as a reducing and residual service,

49

tends to deal with the most vulnerable and damaged young people; many of whom arrive in this environment 'in crisis', as the result of things going badly wrong in their birth family home or because of placement breakdown elsewhere within the care system. Around a quarter of young people in care are likely to have special educational needs (often social, emotional and behavioural difficulties) and they may already have problems with school attendance and with their level of academic and other achievements. An available bed in a residential home may not necessarily be anywhere near an existing school or educational placement, leading to long taxi journeys in order to attend lessons (at best) or further disengagement from the educational system (at worst). Children in residential care have often experienced foster care and a number of placement breakdowns, again adding to existing risk. Connected to this latter point, Darker and colleagues (2008, p 144) found that 'offending behaviour was associated with higher numbers of placements'.

Darker and colleagues (2008) note a correspondence between risk factors associated with offending behaviour and those associated with coming into care. So, added to the well-known risks relating to difficult family circumstances (often rooted in disadvantaged neighbourhoods), poor educational engagement and achievement, and mental health and behavioural problems experienced by many children entering residential care, it is argued that the particular context of this form of care can add to the mix. Specifically, the nature of relationships (both between the young people themselves, and between care staff and young people) and the level of adult surveillance in residential care may mean that young people are more likely to come to the attention of the criminal justice system for behaviour that may be dealt with without recourse to the law in a home environment (Taylor, 2003; Home Office, 2004). Certainly the Crown Prosecution Service advice (CPS, 2006, paras 5 and 6) endorses this view:

> The police are more likely to be called to a children's home than a domestic setting to deal with an incident of offending behaviour by an adolescent. Specialists should bear this in mind when dealing with incidents that take place in a children's home.... A criminal justice disposal, whether a prosecution, reprimand or warning, should not be regarded as an automatic response to offending behaviour by a looked after child, irrespective of their criminal history.

The potential for criminalising *any* group of young people is pertinent to the focus of this chapter, given the number of young people in the general population who admit to offending behaviour in self-report surveys and given the level of surveillance to which young people in residential care are subject. Surveys of young people in mainstream schools show that around a quarter report offending behaviour in a one-year period (see, for example, MORI, 2005; Wilson et al, 2006). So, if adults in a professional role are around troublesome young people, the potential for detecting a crime can be increased.

Relationships between children's homes and the police

At the time of the fieldwork, the local authority children's department had developed a protocol with the police that encouraged officers to consider whether an RJ approach would be suitable in relation to offences committed 'in and around the immediate vicinity of Children's Homes by children resident at the homes'. The protocol advised that the suitability of using the RJ approach would depend on:

> ... the seriousness of the incident, the victims' opinion and the perpetrator's willingness to acknowledge responsibility... Where a minor incident occurs, the police are not notified and it is dealt with by the Children's Home, there is no requirement for a crime to be recorded under NCRS [National Crime Reporting System]. (Local authority internal document)

The devil was, of course, in the detail of this protocol and was dependent on whether individual officers had read it, understood it, supported its values and purpose and knew how to use it in their response.

The nature of relationships with and contact between the police and children's homes were apparent in a number of ways. All homes had some contact and relationship with a local beat police officer (and this was actively encouraged by both services); all had contact in relation to children going missing; most had some contact in relation to extreme behaviour; and most had contact in relation to offending behaviour. In most children's homes, managers described relationships with the police as 'pretty good' in the main or at least 'generally OK', although it was emphasised that there were individual officers who were less than supportive when called in relation to an incident. Problems encountered included the reluctance of police officers to come on certain occasions – situations where particular police officers had made it obvious that they thought staff should expect some level of violence in their job and should not be calling the police. Reflecting on the relatively quiet and affluent location of one home, the manager said that "One officer finds us hard work, we're a bit of a thorn in his side." On the other hand, she acknowledged that another officer had shown sympathy towards staff and was quoted as saying "I couldn't do your job."

Care staff highlighted cases where things had been especially problematic. For example, in one home, staff reported waiting three hours for a 999 emergency response and felt that such a delay was unacceptable. They had also experienced occasions when they felt that the police had forgotten they were dealing with children and had been heavy-handed. In contrast, elsewhere staff reported that when the police had arrived in response to one incident, officers had commented on the distance of the home from the nearest police station (20 minutes' drive), saying that given the problematic behaviour of some of the young people, the home needed direct access to patrol cars in order to ensure a quicker response in dangerous situations. Reference to high-profile events and examples of inappropriate calls (from care staff) or problematic responses (from the police) were usually followed by a comment that 'things were generally OK'. One particular incident, where staff called the police because a young person threw a mug at them, was referred to both by the police and local authority senior managers as an example of involving the police too readily and as an instance where birth parents would not have called the police and risked criminalising their child. The veracity, detail and context of the mug-throwing event were not considered; rather, it was there to make a point about care staff and their lack of proportionality.

Indeed, as we shall see later in this chapter, the police were called out on numerous occasions to all the nine open children's homes (but rarely to the secure unit). The local authority staff and police often focused on behavioural and control issues in relation to such incidents when in reality the most common reason for these call-outs was because children had gone missing. Part of the problem was said to be that residential care environments do not (and cannot) operate like ordinary homes. For example, children in care homes cannot be given a key to their accommodation and as a result they would sometimes stay out rather than return at the time specified by staff.

'Mispers' and 'unauthorised absence'

A significant recording and risk management issue, for both care staff and the police, was posed by young people going missing (recorded by the police as 'mispers') or not returning to the home despite staff knowing their whereabouts ('unauthorised absence'). As one manager said:

> "Mispers' create a phone call from us, then a visit for us to take the form [to the police], a phone call to say the young person has returned. [A visit from the police when the young person returned.] So, for each young person that is four calls, or contacts. If you have three young people in a day, that's 12 contacts.'

Some staff were aware that if a young person was recorded as 'missing', this could lead to a chronology of what could be, or be seen to be, risky behaviour that might ultimately result in the young person being admitted to secure accommodation. As already noted, when young people stayed out all night it was sometimes because staff wanted them home earlier than they were prepared to return. On occasions when staff knew where they were and had confirmed this with the young person, the incident might be recorded as an 'unauthorised absence' (UA). As already highlighted, the context of residential care has helped to create this situation: young people cannot be given a key and if they return very late they may end up in conflict with staff who cannot go to bed until they return but are still required to be up early for work the next morning. These problems were exacerbated by the fact that many of the fieldwork homes were in relatively rural locations, poorly served by public transport, while the young people in care were often from urban environments and used to much more freedom than their current circumstances would allow. All this added up to a situation that increased some of the risks to the young people and contributed to staff stress.

'Mispers' and 'UA' were a particularly significant issue in some of the homes for older teenagers. For example, at the time of a research visit to one home, five of the six young people resident had been recorded as 'missing' or 'UA' on the previous night and in another, three of the five young people resident had been recorded as 'missing' or 'UA' on the previous night. However, in both homes, staff made a clear distinction between young people who were really *missing* (in the sense that they had no idea where they might be) and young people who were classed as 'UA' (in the sense that staff knew where they were). In reality, staff reported having to make judgements on an individual basis, based on age and risk, as the following quotes illustrate:

> 'One of our kids is a missing person officially because we have to, because legally we have to. She's 14 years old. But, we keep in contact and inform the police, we spoke to her yesterday ... she wasn't coming back, but would come back today and so we passed that information on.... We went round to the mother who is a very un-cooperative person ... had we known she was round her son's [that is, the brother of the young person] we would have put her down as an unauthorised absence.'

> 'If we know where they are, particularly with older girls, we go for "unauthorised absence" [rather than a missing person's report]. We make our decisions based on risk.... If we have the staff to do it we will go and search for them before putting them down as a missing person.'

The dynamic of a particular group of young people was said to be important in relation to whether children 'went missing' and this could also relate to the behaviour of a particular individual. For example, the manager of a long-stay unit (for younger children aged 9-13 years) that did not have any young people 'going missing' at the time of a field research visit, reflected on a previous situation concerning an unsettled young girl:

> '... when [she] first came here, she used to abscond on a regular basis and so it depends on the individual and the group dynamics ... initially she was absconding on almost a daily basis. She hasn't for over a year now.'

Calling the police because of behavioural control issues

Managers made the distinction between behavioural problems and criminal behaviour:

> 'We are quite clear that it's not the police's job to manage the kid's behavioural problems, that's our job. There is a line between behavioural problems and committing crime.'

Assaults on staff were said to be a key reason for calling the police, as one manager explained in relation to a young man:

> 'I asked him to come into the room and talk through the violent incidents. Within ten minutes I had been punched three times and head-butted twice. I said to the staff, "Enough is enough, call the police." I said I am making a complaint against this lad, he's too high risk, he's too dangerous for this environment; basically [the police] are going to take him away and I am going to refuse his re-admission. I phoned my line manager who was in total agreement ... [he] went into [the secure unit] and to court the day after.'

When calling the police, a further distinction was made between young people who wanted to and could change their behaviour, those who were distressed and out of control, and those who 'wilfully' (possibly threateningly) chose to be very destructive and smash things up in the home:

> 'If you have a child who is going to change their behaviour we will try and avoid it [police involvement]. Children who have smashed things in the unit because they are upset, perhaps because their mother has just said something unpleasant to them ... we wouldn't be looking to prosecute for smashed windows. But if a young person is saying "If you don't give me what I want I am going to smash this television," and if you then say, "If you smash that television the consequences will be ..." and they are still going to do it, then we probably would be looking to prosecute. But I would discuss this with the service manager and that would be part of the plan for that child.'

One home had called the police to get them to take away a young person because of the level of damage they were doing to the home. It was said (in relation to the police) that in such situations "some can't understand why they are called out". In other words, the police sometimes had the view that such order issues could and should be dealt with by staff.

Restorative justice: the implicit message

Both managers and care staff were aware of the way police call-outs could be interpreted, both generally by senior managers in children's services and by inspectors, as well as specifically in relation to the implementation of an RJ approach. It is interesting to note in this respect that a reduction in the number of police call-outs was viewed as a key measure of 'success' in Littlechild's (2003) research (referred to in Chapter One) in the implementation of RJ in a single children's residential home.

In contrast to wider debates about the 'criminalisation' of children in care, several managers and staff groups clearly felt that the courts were sometimes too lenient with individuals, which not only gave children a confusing message about what they could 'get away with', but also left staff feeling let down after an assault. Staff were often very animated about this issue. Several managers said that it was the right of staff to call the police when they felt threatened, but a few also said that there was an implicit message against resorting to police call-outs in the RJ approach. As one manager said:

'I think that's something that staff felt quite threatened by with the RJ [approach].'

One manager, describing a particular assault suffered by a member of the care staff, said that the charges made against the young person were dropped because it was 'not in the public interest' to pursue a prosecution. In the manager's view, this meant that the young man who had carried out the assault had learned that it was acceptable to assault people and that in effect "he'd got away with it". This manager went on to say that:

'There comes a time when a clear message has to be given ... it wasn't so much that he has hit someone, it was the whole picture, somebody needed to put in some strong boundaries.'

He described how:

'I'm taking a different kid [to court], who tells me, "Did you hear he went to court the other day and all the charges got dropped?" What a way to find out!'

The general message care staff felt they were being given, both from the RJ training and the department, was 'stop calling the police'. Staff often became particularly animated about this issue during interviews. In certain staff groups, there was an obvious sense that the reality of the behaviour with which they were coping was not understood by some managers in their own department, let alone other agencies. Examples were given of comments said to have been made by judges when a young person was in court as a result of an incident in a children's home. There was often some debate about the right of staff and young people to call the police in relation to an incident, if that was what they saw as appropriate. Staff were clear that young people had the right to have the police called over an incident but that their role as professionals was different – they expected a certain amount of 'hassle' due to the nature of the work, but expressed the view that they also needed to draw the line somewhere. Yet they talked about how they would be viewed 'professionally' if they did call the police. Care staff agreed with managers that sometimes 'a line needed to be drawn' to let young people know that they could not behave in a way that would be seen as criminal 'in the real world'.

Concern was also expressed about the potential for young people to manipulate the use of RJ and the perceived need to use the police as a deterrent:

'I believe young people can pay lip service to RJ to avoid police involvement. There is still tension between police involvement and RJ [that] runs the risk of deterioration of the unit without police deterrent.'

The mix of young people and control issues

Lack of placement choice and an inability to plan admissions in the short-term homes also added to problems of control. This was part of the reason why homes could sometimes be very volatile places, yet also experience extended periods of calm. Some major changes in this respect were observed during the two periods of fieldwork in 2006 and 2007, due in part to particular individuals being placed in the homes at the time. The mix of young people in a home could influence school attendance, which in turn could result in offending behaviour or in young people going missing. Certain individuals could sometimes have a major impact on a home. For example, in one short-term home, the admission of a particularly charismatic individual led to a spate of young people accompanying him to take and drive away vehicles without the owners' consent. In another home, incidents involving a young person who was regularly restrained led to an internal departmental enquiry that engulfed the whole home (staff and residents) for some time. In these situations, the wellbeing of staff and young people could suddenly change for the worse. In a third home, young people had started going missing as a group. The remaining residents were greatly outnumbered by staff, which resulted in them wanting to get out of the home too.

Staff in a home for teenagers gave another example of how problems of control (and associated distress) could be caused by the mix of young people present. In this particular incident, three members of staff and two young women were locked in the staff office waiting for the police to arrive, while a young man was attempting to smash all the windows in an effort to reach them. A similar incident occurred in the same home during one of our research visits, illustrating the way in which volatile behaviour could be presented with little warning: less than half an hour after a relaxed research interview, an incident quickly escalated in relation to a young man's protest about the readmission of another individual with whom he had a major conflict the previous evening. The young man protesting had been assured that he would not have to live with the other young man in the home, but because there was nowhere else for him to go, the home had been directed to take him. The conflict resulted in the police being called and both of the young men involved spending a night in a cell.

Incident records

There are various ways in which residential care staff record significant problems that relate to managing young people's behaviour. One way of getting a picture of the pattern across individual homes and the whole service is through the incident records

(IRs) they complete and send to the local authority. The reason for completing these forms relates to both staff injury and future potential claims against the local authority, as well as any physical contact with or threat from a young person. In other words, completing an IR enables staff to 'cover their backs', either in relation to a potential claim against the local authority or to any allegation that might be made against them by the young people in their care. Staff were keen to emphasise that such records were only completed in relation to particularly nasty (often violent) or significant events and that they could complete IRs 'every five minutes' for some young people if it were just a question of rude, non-compliant or difficult behaviour. When we asked managers what (usually) would have to happen before staff completed an IR, all emphasised a physical intervention or contact between staff and young people, as the following explanation illustrates (note that the mug incident referred to earlier in this Chapter re-emerges here):

> 'They [staff] would do them [IRs] at the time when they have laid hands on children, children have laid hands on each other, or children have made complaints about other children ... lack of resolution to events that need to be recorded ... as a separate record that comes to hand.... We certainly don't record events such as being sworn at or young people kicking a door on the way past ... it would have to be half the crockery cupboard on the floor, not a mug on the floor.'

These incident records were previously called 'violent incident records', with the emphasis very much on aggressive and violent behaviour. Earlier research in this local authority showed that cultures of completion or non-completion of these forms varied across homes at any one point in time and did not always present an accurate picture of the level of problem behaviour presented (Hayden, 1998). However, it is reasonable to surmise that staff awareness of the potential consequences of not recording an event had increased since this earlier research. So, although it is recognised that IRs are an imperfect indication of the behaviour presented across children's homes, they do provide some insights into the type of behaviour staff experience and what they perceive as being significant enough to record.

Our research looked at the pattern of incidents over a seven-year period and across each of the 10 homes in order to try to establish trend data. Figure 4.1 illustrates the trend in total number of IRs across all of the homes involved in the research from 2001-02 to 2006-07. The IRs are collected in financial years (1 April to 31 March). Figure 4.1 illustrates an upward trend in these records from 2000 to 31 March 2005 with a marked reduction (26.4%) over the two-year period to 31 March 2007, following staff training and implementation of the RJ approach (although most of this change was during the first year, 2005-06).

Further analysis of IRs showed great variation in the number of records in all 10 homes over this seven-year period. There was no obvious pattern or trend to the number of IRs by individual home; all homes showed big fluctuations in the number of incidents recorded.

Figure 4.1: Trend in number of incident records (2001-07)

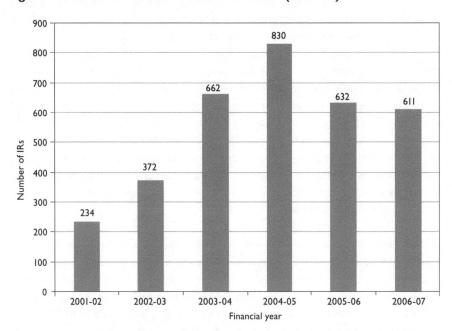

IRs contain information about police involvement in relation to incidents, although these data were not collated at departmental level. They were therefore collated manually from the original forms for a three-year period only, in order to get an indication of how often police were involved. The police were called in 16% (136 of 830) of incidents in 2004-05; 8% (50 of 632) in 2005-06; and 18% (109 of 611) in 2006-07. In general, the police were called in relation to the following situations: a missing child; physical violence towards staff; control issues concerning a young person (either staff were no longer able to hold the young person in the Team-Teach position of 'ground recovery' or staff felt that the young person was at risk of harming themselves or others around them). From reading what was recorded on the IRs, the police were called when the incident was perceived to be at a critical point and the care staff needed extra assistance. However, there were also comments on the IRs about instances where the young person had calmed down before the police arrived. In general, there were very few arrests following police involvement. These latter two situations possibly contributed to police (and departmental) perception that children's homes called the police out inappropriately or too readily.

We conducted further analysis of IRs at the level of individual children during 2006-07. This showed that there were 146 placements involving 115 individual children in that year (some of the 115 children had more than one placement in residential care in the year) and that there were incident records relating to seven in ten (80, 69.6%) of these children. This figure presents some idea of the prevalence of behaviour that was perceived by care staff to be highly problematic and in many cases was also threatening, aggressive or 'violent.'

Further analysis of these data established that particularly problematic behaviour appeared to be concentrated around individuals (also apparent in the earlier research; see Hayden, 1998). Individual case study data were gathered from the IRs on the young person who had the highest number of IRs in each of the homes during the same year (2006-07). These 10 children had 199 IRs (or around a third of all records, 32.6%) over this one-year period. Six of the young people were male and four female and their length of stay ranged from 15 days to 12 months. One in five of these IRs (40, 20%) involved the police and a similar proportion involved violence towards staff. In several units one individual accounted for up to half the IRs in the one-year period. The number of IRs per young person ranged from six to 59, with the higher number being recorded within an 11-month period. (There was an even higher number of IRs for one girl (99) in the case studies reported in Chapter Seven.)

A 'restorative meeting' was one possible outcome that could be recorded on an IR. This was a relatively recent introduction on the IR forms. Analysis of IRs for 2006-07 showed that only 74 (12.1%) recorded a 'restorative meeting' as an outcome. Discussion with staff on this matter highlighted a number of things. For example, the use of the word 'meeting' precluded recording some of the more informal uses of RJ (Chapter Five illustrates that informal uses of RJ were more common than a 'meeting'), and the timing of the use of a restorative approach might mean that it was disconnected from the specific record (which may be some time later, when it was felt to be appropriate). In other words, there are a number of reasons why IRs did not capture the extent to which RJ approaches may have been used in relation to these incidents. Analysis of the issue that led to a restorative meeting being called showed that 'violence towards staff' was a factor in around two thirds of cases (47, 64.4%). 'Violence towards property' was recorded in nearly half of these cases (33, 45.2%). Staff injury was recorded in around one in five incidents leading to a restorative meeting (16, 21.6%).

Police records

Records of calls to the police from children's homes were available for the same time period as IRs. These records were available for calendar years and show a peak of 2,252 calls in 2006 and a marked decrease (28.2%) in calls in 2007. It is interesting to reflect on these data; these calls are in effect to 10 addresses in the county. They show an average of 225.2 calls per home in 2006 and 161.5 calls per home in 2007. From the point of view of the police, this constitutes a massive amount of resources (even after the decrease) and explains their willingness to participate in the RJ steering group and develop a protocol with children's services.

The reduction in the number calls to the police in 2007 can only partly be explained by the closure of two units in early 2007 (mentioned in Chapter Three). Other units had also been closed during the whole period. However, even after adding the equivalent number of calls (for the whole of 2006) from the two units that were

Figure 4.2: Trend in calls to the police (2001-07)

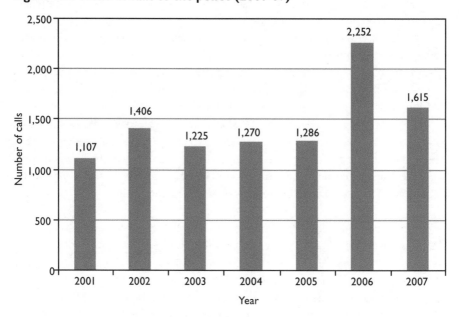

closed in early 2007 to the 2007 total (making a total of 1,974 for 2007, rather than 1,615), this still represents fewer calls to the police in 2007 compared with 2006. As with the IRs, trend data on the number of calls made to the police from individual homes varied across the seven years of data, more so in the case of certain homes. The pattern across units did *not* in general mirror the incident reports. This partly relates to further analysis of the reasons why the police were called. As the data below illustrate, calls to the police are most often related to 'mispers' and UAs. Going missing or UA was a stronger feature of open homes for teenagers and, at times, of the girls' home.

Together, 'mispers' and UAs from children's homes accounted for nearly two thirds (62.4%) of the calls to the police from these homes between 2001 and 2007. Information calls (where information was exchanged about a child – not to report an offence but often to do with whereabouts; for example, found after being reported as missing) accounted for a further 15.6% of all calls. In total, 78% of all calls from children's homes to the police during this period related to these three issues ('mispers', 'UAs' and information calls).

Almost all of the rest of the calls ('other', 2,229 or 21.9%) relate to criminal and nuisance behaviour, most frequently theft, assault, vehicle-related offences, public order offences and so on (see Figure 4.4). Interestingly, there was very little evidence of police call-outs for the various conflicts or keeping-order issues recorded in IRs. In other words, calls to the police give an indication of a different aspect of behaviour (and behaviour management issues) in children's homes; these records generally focus on concerns about the whereabouts of children and young people ('mispers' and UAs), information exchange and offending behaviour. Concern for the young person's

Figure 4.3: Main reasons for calls to the police (2001-07)

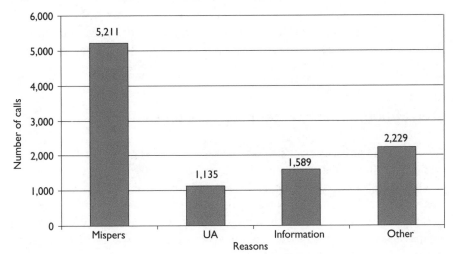

Figure 4.4: Criminal and nuisance calls to the police (2001-07)

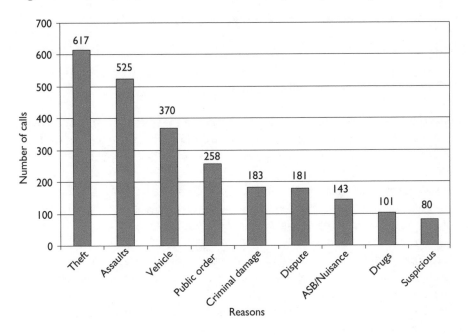

welfare (other than 'mispers' and UAs) made up only a minority of calls to the police (156, or 1.5% of calls made between 2001 and 2007).

Although police records indicated that criminal and nuisance behaviour was the reason for calls to the police in around one in five cases, this still amounted to a large volume of calls from a single address, averaging at 223 calls per home over seven years, or 32 calls per year. The calls were most concentrated in the seven open homes that catered for teenagers, with relatively few calls to the two homes for younger children (aged 9-13 years) and even less for the secure children's home.

Out-of-hours management support service

An out-of-hours management support service was piloted during the field research (2006 and 2007), so this organisational data was also available for analysis. This service was based on managers of residential homes being part of an 'out-of-hours' rota that was available to care staff across the county. In effect, this meant managers being on call in the evenings, at nights and at weekends. There were clear documented criteria for the use of this service and managers were expected to log all calls for the period they covered. Some of the criteria for staff using this service have a direct bearing on the behavioural and control issues that are the focus of this chapter. Top of the list of the criteria for calling the out-of-hours service was:

'If staff feel the need to call the police (excluding 999 situations).'

This was followed by:

'Immediately having dealt with a 999 situation.'

Calls to this service averaged at around 12 a week at the start of the service and eight a week at the end of the second period of monitoring. This may not seem like many calls but it could mean one manager being disturbed in the evening or in the middle of the night on several occasions in one week, after which they could be working the following day. Analysis of these data by individual home again showed marked changes in the volume of use of this service by individual homes across this time period, mirroring the kinds of changes shown in the analysis of IRs.

Interviews with managers helped illuminate the use of this service: they advised that caution should be used in interpreting what it meant. For example, certain homes were reported to prefer to call their own manager (in preference to the duty manager) and therefore these calls would not appear on the out-of-hours log. Furthermore, as one manager said:

'Use of this service is not a meaningful indicator of the risks managed.'

Thus, although the records showed a decrease in usage of the service between 2006 and 2007, managers did not think this necessarily indicated a calmer living and working environments in residential homes.

Figure 4.5 is based on an analysis of 86 calls made during an 11-week period in 2007. Only eight of these calls were viewed as unnecessary by the manager overseeing this monitoring. It is clear from this analysis that children going missing ('mispers') is the reason for a call to this service in nearly half of the calls (40, 46.5%) made. One in six calls (14, 16.3%) were to do with staffing issues. Children in custody, police 999 calls and other contacts with the police together account for almost one in five

Figure 4.5: Out-of-hours service: reasons for calling (2007)

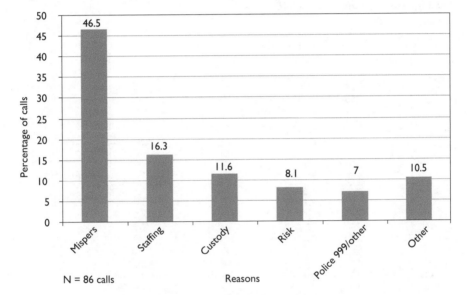

N = 86 calls   Reasons

calls (16, 18.6%), which when added to the 'mispers' calls indicates that around two thirds of the calls made (56, 65.1%) are likely to involve contact with the police. 'Risk management' (7, 8.1%) and 'other' reasons (9, 10.5%) accounted for the rest of the calls.

Trend in number and rate of children offending

Figures 4.6 and 4.7 show the number and proportion of children in care for more than a year and who have a record of offending, over the period 2001-07. Figure 4.10 also illustrates that the overall trend is an increase in the number of children in care for more than a year. The data in Figures 4.6 and 4.7 cover the whole service for looked after children (that is *not* just children in residential homes) and is taken from annual returns to the Department for Children, Schools and Families (and previously to the Department of Health). The graphs illustrate a fluctuation in the number and proportion of children offending.

As we noted in Chapter Two, performance data in local authorities focuses on all children looked after for a year. It does not differentiate by type of care environment and can therefore be misleading. In this local authority, the percentage of young people who had a record of a final warning or conviction in a one-year period fluctuated between 6.7% and 11.8% over the 2001-07 period, with a mean of 9.6% (or near to the national average in 2007). Figure 4.6, however, reminds us once again that *most children in care do not offend*. Further, the number of children that account for

Figure 4.6: Trend in number of offenders, compared with all children in care for more than a year (2001-07)

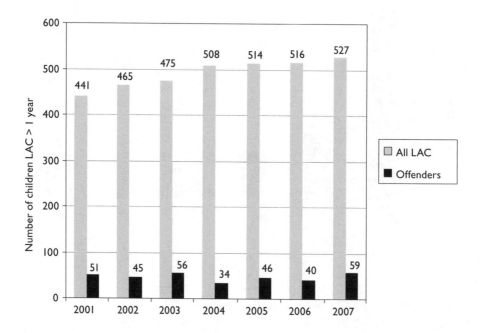

any change in the percentage offending is very small, ranging from 39 to 59 children per year across the time period investigated. As noted in Chapter Three, internal monitoring within the local authority showed that the largest proportion of those with a record of offending were in residential care. This is further illustrated by the number of young people offending in the cohort and case file studies, reported on in Chapter Seven.

Overall, the data presented in this chapter illustrates a great deal of difficult to manage behaviour across children's residential care. Seven in 10 children (69.6%) had an incident record in 2006-07 and most homes had a young person about whom there were multiple records. Over 10,000 calls were made to the police between 2001 and 2007, or well over 1,000 calls a year. Six in 10 of these calls (62.4%) related to children

Figure 4.7: Comparing trends in percentage of children with a record of offending: national and case study local authority (2001-07)

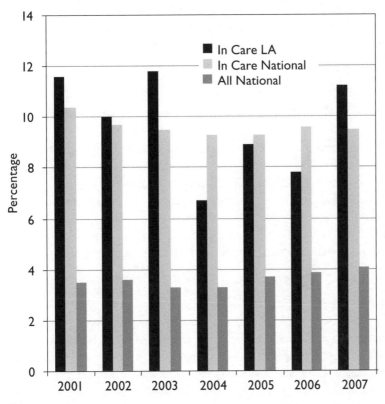

Notes:

In care LA = percentage of young people in care with a record of offending in the case study local authority.

In care national = percentage of young people in care with a record of offending nationally.

All national = percentage of all young people with a record of offending nationally.

Source: Local authority and DCSF data from annual 'Outcomes' reports; see www.dcsf.gov.uk

going missing or to an unauthorised absence. There are different peaks and patterns across the children's homes over the seven-year period in relation to IRs and police call-outs. The out-of-hours service is also dominated by missing person concerns in nearly five in 10 calls (46.5%). Offending and nuisance behaviour is clearly apparent in IRs and calls to the out-of-hours service, as well as in calls to the police. Police records indicate this to be the issue in about a fifth of calls recorded; theft, assaults, vehicle-related offences and public order offences are the most common issues recorded.

The overall number and proportion of children offending (of those looked after for more than a year) fluctuated across the 2001-07 period. The rate in 2007 is almost the same as in 2001 and 2003. It remains higher than the national average for children in care for more than a year, which has decreased slightly over the same time period. It is also interesting to note the increase in the rate for 'all children' between 2004 and 2007. These data covers the whole service and the great majority of looked after children who are placed in foster care. However, we know that a large proportion of official records of offending behaviour are concentrated among children in the residential care environment.

Is children's residential care a 'criminogenic' environment?

This chapter gives some indication of the extent and nature of the problematic and offending behaviour in these 10 children's residential homes that was significant enough to be recorded. As several staff said during the course of the field research, there were countless incidents that were aggressive or threatening; what got recorded were the more high-profile events, where staff believed it was necessary to record what had happened. The interest of staff in trying to develop new ways of managing difficult behaviour was based on the need to reduce the all too numerous opportunities for conflict.

Despite the best efforts of most staff to avoid calling the police unless they felt it was absolutely necessary, the frequency of incidents involving children going missing was very high and automatically resulted in police involvement. Furthermore, the circumstances of young people (particularly older teenagers) in residential care tended to represent a mutually reinforcing set of risks that could be made worse, rather than ameliorated, by the care experience. The mix of residents in some homes for teenagers, the number of young people going missing overnight or who were out of full-time education and as the distress and disruption associated with the care experience combined to produce a situation where offending behaviour was common. Indeed, when we look closely at individual children (see Chapter Seven), we see that around three quarters of the children in the cohort study (35, 76.1%) had a record of offending, with most of these young people having a record of offending in a one-year period of monitoring. In other words, it becomes more pertinent to ask what prevented the others from having 'a record' too. We will return to this issue in more depth in Chapter Seven.

Finally, it must be emphasised that caution should always be applied when interpreting organisational data and official records, as levels of recording may be affected by organisational issues such as home closures and refurbishments, as well as the priority accorded to monitoring and recording and the organisational pressures arising from calling the police (or not). Further, as one of the quotes above indicates, these data do not illustrate the risks managed by staff. Having said this, the data in this chapter do show a reduction in the use of three of the four types of organisational record: IRs peaked in 2004-05 and then decreased; police calls peaked in 2006 and decreased in 2007; and calls to the out-of hours service decreased between the 2006 and 2007 monitoring periods. Taken together, this suggests some positive change in the way that problematic behaviour was managed within homes. The overall pattern in these findings is in keeping with Littlechild's (2003) research on one residential home; this reported fewer incidents and police call-outs following the introduction of an RJ approach. Our research also supports the evidence from a Home Office (2004) study, which included the use of a protocol between the police and social services and resulted in staff in children's homes taking greater responsibility for incidents, rather than calling the police. If this sort of change is interpreted in a way that fits with the underpinning philosophy of a restorative approach (see Christie, 1977, and Chapter One of this volume), the evidence of a reduction in resorting to external support can be seen as indicative of homes 'owning' more of their conflicts. Table 4.1 summarises the overall pattern of evidence from these four sources.

Table 4.1: Overall trends in organisational data

Organisational data (source and purpose)	% change: 2006-07	Overall trend: 2001-07
Percentage and number of children offending (recorded offending)	Increased from 7.8% to 11.2% (from 40 to 59 children)	Level of offending similar in 2007 (11.2%) to 2001 (11.6%). Fluctuated between these years
Incident records (particularly violence, aggression and physical interventions)	Decreased by 3.3%	Overall trend was upward between 2001 and 2004-05, reducing in the last two years (between 2005 and 2007) by 26.4%
Police call-outs (most often 'mispers' and 'UAs', also offending)	Decreased by 28.2%	Overall trend was upward between 2001 and 2006, reducing in the last year
Calls to the out-of-hours service (most often 'mispers', then staffing; or custody, risk or 999 call)	Decreased by 22.4%	Data only available for periods in 2006 and 2007

Using restorative justice: manager and care staff views

5

Introduction

This chapter is based on the experiences, views and perceptions of managers and care staff. It focuses mainly on staff and managers' use of restorative justice (RJ) in managing the kinds of behaviours outlined in the previous chapter and their assessment of the effectiveness of this approach. Their views were collated in four main ways: by questionnaires administered in autumn 2006 and again in autumn 2007; by structured group discussions with care staff within the same two time periods; by individual interviews with unit managers, again in the same two periods; and, throughout the research by participation in staff meetings that included presentations of interim findings to managers and key staff involved in implementing the RJ approach. This level of interaction with practitioners helped maintain interest in the research and ensure the relevance of questions asked. Fewer staff completed questionnaires or interviews in 2007 (81 staff), compared with 2006 (113 staff). The main reasons for this were the closure of two of the 10 homes by autumn 2007, working time directives that limited staff availability in some units, and staff vacancies in one unit.

Staff assessment and use of the restorative justice approach

Administering the same questionnaire at two different times meant that it was possible to track any overall change in the assessment and use of the RJ approach. Questionnaires used a Likert scale of 24 statements and asked staff to report on the last instance in which they had used the restorative approach. The Likert scale was short, with four possible ratings for each statement – 1 representing 'strongly disagree' and 4 representing 'strongly agree' – as we wanted staff to indicate strength of agreement or disagreement and avoid any 'sitting on the fence' by having a middle rating on a five-point scale. Therefore, the higher the rating, the more staff agreed with a particular statement. Responses to statements were grouped into four main categories (see Table 5.1): staff – own practice and competence; using RJ with young people; the impact of RJ; and staff assessment of the practice and understanding of colleagues. Table 5.1 illustrates the broad grouping and direction of change shown by staff responses in the two time periods. The table shows that most care staff, when reporting on their own practice and competence, indicated positive change and found the RJ approach in tune with their professional practice. They also believed that they understood the principles of RJ, they felt confident in using the approach, they found RJ compatible with using the established Team-Teach approach and so on. The areas where there was no progress or even some slight backward movement mostly related to staff assessments of the practice and understanding of their colleagues, including the resolution of conflicts between young people and staff.

The lowest rating given both times the questionnaire was completed was for assessment of whether the RJ approach was viewed as 'a tough option' for young people. This was included because advocates of RJ (such as former chief constable of Thames Valley Police, Charles Pollard) are keen to emphasise that RJ is not an easy option for young people; rather, it is presented by some advocates of RJ as a 'tough option'. The RJ training organisation in our case study local authority also took this view in the documentation supporting their approach. This is something that perhaps needs to be taken into account when considering alternatives to using RJ; it may indeed be more valid within the more formal part of the criminal justice system (see later comments from staff), although the way in which RJ is seen as 'a tough option', and why, needs some further thought and clarification in relation to its use in children's residential care. It may be that whether or not RJ is perceived as a 'tough option' is not really relevant or meaningful in this setting (in the way it was used and in the situations it was addressing). Interestingly, the introduction of an additional statement in 2007 about whether RJ was 'a tough option for staff' achieved a very similar rating to the statement when applied to young people.

Assessments of the impact of using RJ were very mixed and are discussed in more length later in this chapter, in relation to what staff said during interviews and discussions. The main point to make here is that although staff overall were nearer to agreement about resulting improvements in homes as living and working environments and in relation to conflict resolution than they were to reporting no change, it was clear that some staff expected more immediate and dramatic change than was the case.

In general, managers were more positive than care staff in their assessment of most aspects of using RJ. Where managers were less positive than care staff, this related to their assessment of staff understanding, training and confidence in using RJ, and whether a staff team had a common understanding of the approach. The issue of common understanding also resonated with what staff said about each other. Interestingly, managers were less positive than care staff about whether young people were supportive of the RJ approach being used to resolve conflicts.

Overall, analysis of all staff questionnaires (managers and care staff combined) shows a *positive shift* in staff assessments of the approach over the one year-time period when the approach was being implemented. A paired samples T-test (parametric) was performed to test the hypothesis that there was a positive change in overall staff attitudes towards the approach and its impact between time one (autumn 2006) and time two (autumn 2007). This test showed that overall there was a statistically significant positive change in staff perceptions of the use and impact of RJ from time one (overall mean = 2.87, SD = 0.32) to time two (overall mean = 2.96, SD = 0.37), $t(24) = -3.655$, $p < 0.001$ (two-tailed). In addition, a Wilcoxon signed ranks test (non-parametric) was performed to test the same hypothesis, as the nature of the data and their distribution arguably do not fully meet the criteria needed for the use of a parametric test, as in the T-test. Again, this test showed a significant positive change in staff attitudes (p < 0.002, two-tailed).

Table 5.1: Implementing restorative justice: staff perceptions about its use and impact

Focus of statement	Change: 2006-2007; mean ratings 2007
Staff – own practice and competence Compatibility of RJ with professional practice and other training (eg Team-Teach), staff understanding and confidence in the use of RJ, perceptions of their own fairness	*All positive change in rating* Highest rating (2007): 3.6 (compatibility with professional practice) Lowest rating (2007): 3.23 (staff confidence in using RJ)
Using RJ with young people Young people feel better after RJ, like and understand the approach, see RJ as a 'tough option'	*All positive change in rating* Highest rating: 3.00 (young people feel better) Lowest rating: 2.33 (young people see RJ as a 'tough option')
Impact of using RJ Improved living and working environment, relationships improved, resolving conflict	*Mixed rating* Small positive change (2007): improvements in home as a living environment 2.60, as a working environment 2.53, and in resolving conflicts between young people 2.66 Small negative change (2007): 2.56 resolving conflicts between staff and yps
The practice and understanding of colleagues Fairness of other staff, common understanding of RJ across the home, staff understanding of their own behaviour, resolving conflict between staff	*All slight reductions in rating* Highest rating (2007): 2.99 (common understanding of RJ among staff) Lowest rating (2007): 2.43 (success of RJ in resolving conflicts between staff)

Notes: 1 = strongly disagree; 4 = strongly agree.

The identification of particular implementation issues in the analysis of the questionnaires was explained by comments made in staff and manager interviews. In other words, while an overall positive change in staff attitudes was reported across the service, there were some individual members of staff who had not embraced the implementation of the RJ approach between autumn 2006 and 2007, and this dissenting view was becoming more obvious within staff groups.

How restorative justice was used

In order to try to capture how the RJ approach was being used, staff were asked about how they had last used the RJ approach. To make the responses meaningful and comparable, staff were provided with the diagram and information developed from

Wachtel (1999) and shown in Figure 1.1, Chapter One that shows RJ as a continuum of approaches and asked to indicate which of the five possibilities illustrated the way they used RJ. This continuum had already been piloted with a group of managers and care staff to ensure that it made sense to them. It was known from early meetings with key care staff and managers, as well as from piloting the questionnaire and from internal documents, that a full scripted RJ 'conference' was unlikely to be the most frequently used approach within children's residential care. Furthermore, as questionnaires were administered face to face during fieldwork we could ensure that staff understood what was being asked.

Figure 5.1 shows that RJ was most often used informally, as in a style of questioning or statement about a young person's behaviour, or in a situation of minor conflict. 'Impromptu conferences' generally involved one member of staff (occasionally two) sitting down with the young people involved as quickly as they could after an event. Formal scripted conferences were rare and reserved for the most problematic events. In practice, staff did not make a meaningful distinction between 'large group conferences' and 'formally scripted conferences'. By 2007, there was a further shift towards using more informal RJ approaches, with proportionally more staff using RJ as a style of communication through a 'statement' in 2007 (compared with 2006).

Figure 5.2 illustrates when RJ was last used, with at least half of all staff using the approach within the last week or more recently. However, some change is evident across the two periods of field research, with more staff reporting that the last time they used RJ was 'more than a week ago' in 2007 compared with 2006.

Figure 5.1: How the restorative justice approach was used (2006, 2007)

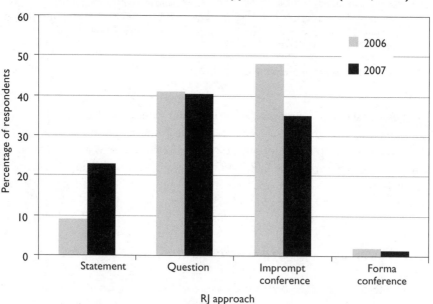

2006: N = 109; 2007: N = 78

Figure 5.2: When restorative justice was last used (2006, 2007)

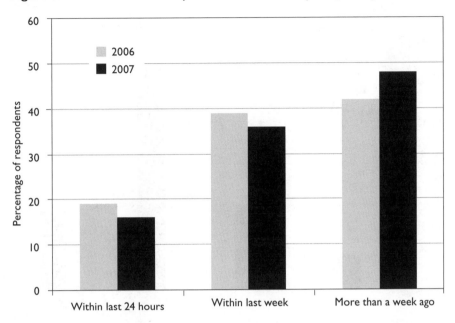

2006: N = 110; 2007: N = 79

Figure 5.3 shows that overall staff felt that RJ 'moved a situation or problem forward' at least to some extent in relation to the incident they were reporting, with only a minority indicating that RJ did not move things forward at all. By 2007, there was an increase in the small number of staff who believed that the RJ approach did not help ('not at all') to move forward a situation or problem; however, there was also an increase in the most positive assessments ('to a great extent'). This change seems to reflect the differences in staff groups, already noted in the staff rating of their colleagues (and illustrated in staff interviews). The mean rating for both years is very similar and is on the side of positive change.

Contact and discussions with staff, both in fieldwork and in other meetings, illustrated that the concept of reparation was relatively underdeveloped (and not always fully understood by some staff) as part of the RJ process. Figure 5.4 shows that although some form of reparation was apparent in over half the RJ encounters reviewed, the use of reparation did not increase between the two periods of field research. Whether some form of reparation was deemed possible or appropriate to the situations in which RJ was used within children's residential care was a theme that featured in most staff interviews.

Figures 5.5 and 5.6 illustrate who staff identified as the 'victims' and 'offenders' in a situation where an RJ approach was used. Figure 5.6 illustrates that in both 2006 and 2007 RJ approaches were mostly used to resolve issues between staff and young people.

Figure 5.3: Whether restorative justice moved a situation or problem forward (2006, 2007)

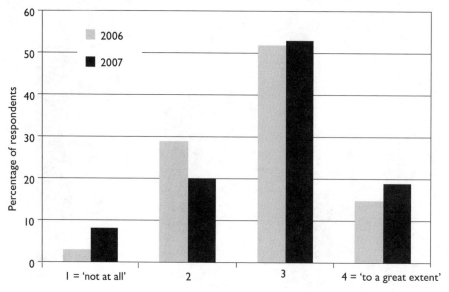

2006: N = 92; 2007: N = 64

2006: Mean = 2.79; 2007: Mean = 2.83

Figure 5.4: Whether reparation followed the use of restorative justice (2006, 2007)

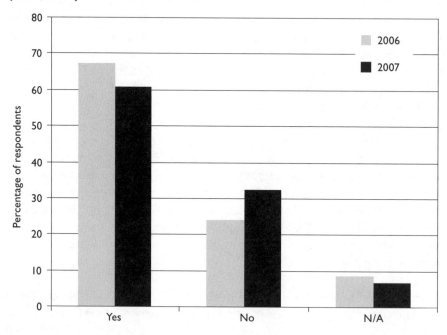

2006: N = 104; 2007: N = 74

Figure 5.5: Who were the 'victims'? (2006, 2007)

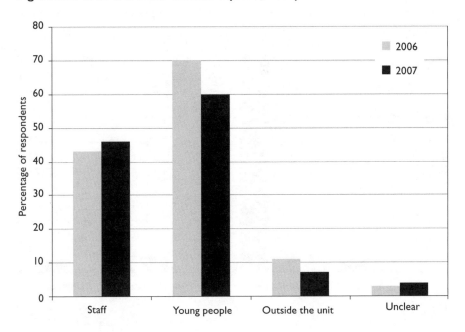

006: N = 79 2007: N = 80

Note: Percentage does not add up to 100% as some incidents had more than one victim.

Figure 5.6 also shows that, from the staff perspective, young people are most often the 'offenders' in the situations where RJ is used.

Recording and evidencing the use of any impact of RJ was an ongoing focus of discussion during the research, with managers wanting more systematic evidence and some staff feeling that there were simply too many potential incidents to record.

Assessing the overall impact of the restorative justice approach

As explained earlier in this volume, key to the purpose of adopting an RJ approach was the aim of resolving conflict, reducing offending behaviour and improving homes as working and living environments. We have already addressed overall staff assessment of these issues through their questionnaire responses; what follows is an account of staff comments made during interview. We deal specifically with recorded evidence about offending and other problem behaviour in more detail in Chapters Four and Seven. A reduction in offending behaviour was a high priority in terms of measurable change (partly because of performance management targets), yet this was known to be a highly complex issue affected by all kinds of variables (children's behaviour, the influence of peers, care staff response, police response and so on) and other contextual issues, not least changes in the residential service itself during the period

Figure 5.6: Who were the 'offenders'? (2006, 2007)

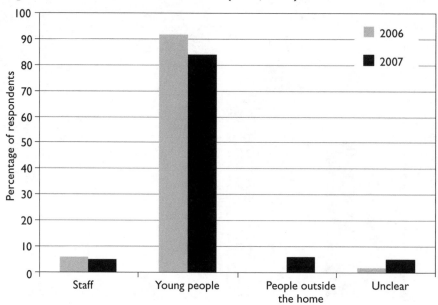

2006: N = 113; 2007: N = 80

of research. When assessing the overall impact of using RJ, a common response from care staff, as well as several home managers, was that RJ was a useful tool, one among others, but one that could not (and should not) be used to resolve all conflicts.

So, while managers were supportive of the RJ approach, they were also cautious about their expectations of measurable change. Some of the reported impact of using RJ was said to be in relation to helping to address staff feelings of powerlessness in the face of highly problematic behaviour. As one manager said:

> 'Some staff feel less powerless [using RJ]. They know the criminal route doesn't bring the consequences wanted. It takes forever to get to court and they get solicitors who if they can't deny it [whatever the young person is accused of] seek to minimise it. [The criminal justice route] takes away taking responsibility for your actions.'

Simply having RJ as an alternative way of resolving issues in the residential setting was seen as of value. An example was given of a member of staff who was assaulted by a young person choosing RJ, rather than the criminal justice route, as a way of responding to the incident. The rationale behind this was described as follows:

> 'He wanted a method of resolving things more quickly.... Because [staff] have to continue working with children they need quite quick resolutions.'

As well as valuing the approach, however, many staff shared the sentiment that:

'It hasn't had a major impact, not a major impact, it is a useful tool.'

It was also noted that:

'The staff are slower to think about sanctions and quicker to think about problem solving.'

Managers had some issues with staff expectations and staff members' assessment of the usefulness of the RJ approach. Some expected the approach to 'work' because of the message conveyed in the training, so while RJ provided a coherent approach, staff could be frustrated when there was no immediate change in a young person's behaviour:

'It has got staff together ... but they are more likely to say, "It doesn't work" with RJ than with a sanction.'

On the other hand, when staff were asked to reflect on an incident where they thought RJ had 'worked', a more complex picture could emerge:

'After a really serious incident I was involved in I used the RJ approach, but it was weeks and weeks later ... we really talked about feelings.... I guess it worked, because they haven't pushed it that far again.'

In general, the informal use of RJ was seen as more useful in the residential care context:

'...the formal conference is an absolute nightmare, in terms of resources, getting people to buy into it, it's not very user-friendly ... [but] the informal RJ works great.'

Like managers, care staff often said that RJ was one of a number of ways in which they responded to conflict or difficult behaviour; indeed, some staff groups were a little bemused as to why there was so much emphasis on RJ. A typical response was as follows:

'A useful tool, but not the answer to everything.'

At the same time, several staff in most homes could see the potential for further development of the approach:

'It feels like a lost opportunity ... [we need] more opportunity for specific discussion on the practical use of RJ approaches. Its themes are central to what we do, but we need assistance to incorporate relevant structures. A key individual/consultant attached to a home to work alongside staff for a month or so and look at the practical issues. We are so close, but a huge step away from success.'

'Certainly not a quick fix. Something young people and staff need to continually work at. Starting to bring about positive change despite being difficult to measure!'

Staff resistance to using an RJ approach

A common theme in individual interviews with managers, and one that was often clearly evident in the dynamics of staff group interviews (especially during the second period of field research in autumn 2007), was the open criticism or resistance to the RJ approach by a minority of staff. Managers wanted to see more consistency across staff groups, although they could also see some evidence of ongoing change and positive development within their teams. Typical comments were:

'It has lots of potential but its frustrating getting *all* staff on board.'

'Refresher training has moved a few more individuals – RJ is encroaching further into the group, but not as fast as I would like.'

However, in certain units, even some senior staff were viewed as actively unhelpful; they did not record what they did, even when they used RJ, and could also be critical of others using the approach:

'He was critical of his colleague who chose not to report a child to the police [after an assault] and used RJ instead. He said that gave the child the message that they could assault staff.'

'I feel that there are still some staff that see RJ as an easy option for kids.'

'Some staff are still reluctant to use an RJ approach and this is identified as a training need ...[they need staff development] ... and to complete the refresher course. The yps [young people] view it as something that happens when they have done something wrong, I want it to be a daily form of interaction between staff and yps.'

Some managers held the view that RJ is more effort for staff than giving young people a 'sanction'. 'Sanction' was the term used for various forms of 'punishment' or 'consequence' (depending on the underlying behaviour management philosophy most established and supported within a home). So, for example, sending a young person to bed early or not allowing them to watch television was seen as easier for staff than trying to resolve the conflict or problem behaviour.

Nevertheless, there were clear advocates of RJ in all staff teams. It was interesting to see that staff were very willing to air their differences about the approach as a group. Sometimes these 'advocates' could be quite frustrated with their colleagues:

'I feel the staff in my unit are resisting the RJ approach and see it as a soft option and are generally very negative about it. When they do use it, it feels to me that they are only paying lip service to it and have not adequately prepared what they want to get out of it. As an advocate of RJ, I find this attitude incredibly frustrating. There seems to be an inability amongst the staff to understand the principles of RJ. I do feel that part of this inability stems from a desire to not want to know about it.

Some care staff reflected their managers' views in relation to the desire to see a whole-staff approach:

'I feel that RJ could be used a lot more within the unit, but it needs the whole staff team to have a positive attitude to it and use it as part of their everyday practice.'

Practice issues

Managers and care staff often queried the use of the term 'restorative *justice*', particularly in relation to the word 'justice', which was often disliked, but also in relation to whether it was really that different from good professional practice with young people. By autumn 2007, the use of the term 'restorative *approach*' was more common than 'restorative justice'. This did not mean that all aspects of the concept were rejected; it tended to mean that staff were adapting ideas based on RJ to their practice in a residential setting. The idea that RJ was 'something we've always done' was evident in an internal report to the department in 2005 at the time staff were initially trained in the approach, as well as in the first stage of the fieldwork (in autumn 2006). It was again emphasised in the follow-up visits to homes in autumn 2007.

In one home, the manager saw the advantage of having the RJ framework in endorsing existing good practice and enhancing staff confidence, because there was a name and a framework to attach to what they were trying to do:

'For a lot of staff it [RJ] has reinforced existing practice, given it a name ... [but] ... staff are more confident about getting two people in the same place, to talk things through and resolve things. In the past they would have talked to the two young people separately in their rooms, then expected them to walk off and resolve things together afterwards.... It doesn't work that way.... Now staff take people [together] into the quiet area.'

This principle and practice of 'encounter' is central to adopting the spirit of a restorative approach. The idea that problems can be resolved through interaction, facilitated by somebody trained and experienced, was evident in many of the interviews and discussions with staff. Raising the issue of recording the use of RJ was often initially met with the comment that it would be 'too frequent to be meaningful' if all restorative approaches were recorded, but that:

'[It's] OK if it has got as far as sitting down with a couple of young people. Contact sheets are the most obvious place to record these encounters.'

Care staff as a group were more critical about the RJ approach than their managers in a number of ways. They were also likely to emphasise that a range of responses and approaches to resolving conflict and unwanted behaviour were used. For example, in one home, the staff said that they had developed a new incentive scheme to work alongside the RJ approach where young people could, say, earn a ticket to see a professional football match. They felt that they had moved from sanctions to positive approaches to behaviour management. At the same time, staff in some homes reported that 'sanctions' (that were clearly punishments), such as delaying pocket money (for up to 72 hours), removing TVs from bedrooms and turning the electricity off, were also imposed.

Using restorative justice with young people

Interviews with staff in autumn 2007 raised more issues about using RJ with young people than in 2006. It was evident that over time more considerations had arisen. Managers were keen to see children take responsibility for what they had done and some clearly felt that using RJ helped in this process:

'It's helped the children take more responsibility, definitely, definitely.'

A few staff saw RJ as a way of encouraging the development of 'emotional literacy' and saw the whole approach as integral to working with children who had damaging experiences with others.

On the other hand, some managers clearly shared the concerns of certain care staff and therapists (see below) about whether RJ was an appropriate approach with particular children:

'Sometimes the kids don't want to engage.... Asking them to talk about feelings can be too much.... What they were feeling is too complex, they can't identify "anger", "sad", "scared".'

In several units, staff questioned whether RJ was an appropriate approach that could be used meaningfully with all young people in residential care. This observation was supported by therapists working in two of the homes, some of whom had specific concerns. For example, one therapist (who was present during the fieldwork) said of young people in residential care:

'A lot can't empathise. Most have huge issues with shame. They are well defended and will just close down.'

Furthermore, a couple of the young people in the home supported by this therapist had been diagnosed as being on the autistic spectrum, which meant that they found it difficult to show empathy (a feature of this condition). The mix of young people resident in the home – particularly victims and offenders/perpetrators (see from Little, 2000, cited earlier in Chapter Two) – was also seen as highly problematic.

In another home, a member of care staff reported:

'At least one of our young people is unable to participate in RJ. [The] educational psychologist and therapist agree it would be used to further intimidate as they are unable to accept responsibility for their actions.'

Care staff sometimes questioned the motivation of some young people who were willing to participate in an RJ approach:

'Young people are looking to use RJ now, instead of sanctions. They would rather clean the hallway than miss TV.'

'I believe the RJ approach can work in certain conflicts between staff and yps [young people] but not always between yps as most of our children don't want to accept responsibility for their behaviour. They also seem to want an RJ meeting ... [in situations where] they will have to pay for damaged property, as they know they will not have to pay for a small amount.'

The roles of 'victim' and 'offender' were said not to be always obvious in the context of children living together. Concern was expressed that the RJ process had the potential to create victims – individuals who did not feel they were victims without the process. The potential for re-victimisation in RJ meetings was also raised. Both these concerns were in evidence in both periods of fieldwork.

The principle of voluntarism in the restorative justice approach

It became increasingly apparent during the research that the important principle of voluntarism in relation to participation in an RJ approach could be at odds with attempts to adopt a consistent approach to conflict resolution within homes and across children's services. This issue was generally raised by care staff (as opposed to managers) and was apparent in a number of ways, for example, in the way that care staff felt they had to justify why they had *not* used RJ, as opposed to why they had, in the ongoing perception that calling the police was frowned on and in relation to external pressures to participate in RJ meetings from the youth offending team (YOT). As one member of staff said:

'Sometimes we don't feel comfortable about *not* using the restorative approaches.'

This latter comment reflected staff awareness that the RJ approach was imposed to some extent. Certain aspects of the process, such as the option of calling in the police, could make staff feel uncomfortable; indeed, some stated that they 'felt rotten about calling the police'. Yet, as we saw in Chapter Four, the perceived need for support gained by calling the police was seen as an important right of staff, especially when they were the victims in an incident. Furthermore, staff were clear that it was the undisputed right of young people to have the option of calling the police in.

Concern about the way that RJ could become routine with young people and just another process in the care system – even something to which they just paid lip service – is encapsulated in the way that one member of staff referred to the use of RJ as "being RJ'd", "you've been RJ'ed" and "being RJ'ed without the staff [as victim] being present".

External pressures from the YOT meant that staff and young people could feel that they had to participate in meetings that were not necessarily wanted or perceived as useful by the time they were convened. In some cases, this was because another meeting was seen as going over issues that had been sufficiently resolved earlier within the home. The number of people who could be involved in such external meetings was viewed as overwhelming for young people, as the following comment illustrates:

> 'Members of staff had accompanied a young man to a referral order panel after he had asked them to go with him. The two staff members [care staff] were asked to leave the room leaving the young man surrounded by adult professionals and community members.'

Staff in one home particularly wanted to discuss how they felt that 'proper RJ' (that is, a large formal conference or meeting) run by the YOT had felt coercive when a member of staff had been the victim. This member of staff reported feeling pressurised to attend a meeting with the YOT, with themselves in the role of 'victim'. This meeting was arranged a long time after the incident, so much so that the staff member and young person had addressed the incident informally and had moved on, now enjoying a positive relationship. This member of staff stated that they kept getting calls from someone they did not know asking them to attend a conference where the young person's behaviour was to be addressed, despite their insistence that it had already been addressed within the home. The staff member questioned whether the same incident should be discussed over and over again. They also made the point that victims should feel able to decline such 'invitations'. Reflecting on this situation, staff member assessed the RJ approach as:

> '[It's] used well in the unit but outside poorly managed in a formal conference a young person attended – [did] more harm. More informal methods seem to work well.'

Ensuring restorative outcomes

As noted above, the concept of reparation was not always fully understood and the notion of 'restorative outcomes' was probably the least developed aspect of using the RJ approach in the autumn 2006 visits to homes. The feeling that an apology was somehow not enough was a common one; there was also a sense that young people sometimes viewed making an apology as simply paying lip service to a situation. Greater recognition of the value of 'genuine apologies' was more evident in autumn 2007 than autumn 2006. On the other hand, certain managers still felt that the outcomes of some RJ encounters remained largely punitive and sanction-based, resulting in the 'loss of' something (such as watching TV) rather than agreed reparation from young people.

Like some care staff, managers acknowledged that genuine apologies were an important form of reparation. As one manager explained:

> 'We don't expect the kids to apologise unless they mean it. We expect them to be civil…. The kids will say, "I'm not apologising now, because I won't mean it." Our kids quite like that to be honest.'

In one example given during an interview, the presence of a girl from the children's home at an RJ meeting with a neighbouring school where she and some local children had been involved in some unpleasant vandalism was clearly very much appreciated by the school's head teacher. Following the RJ meeting, the head teacher sent a letter to the children's home to say how impressed they had been with the girl coming to apologise in person. Interestingly, the local children who were not resident in the home had not been willing to participate in the meeting.

Both managers and staff often agreed about the need to be more imaginative in the use of restorative outcomes and options, and several managers talked of expanding the use of RJ in various ways, for example, in working with birth parents.

At the same time, as noted above, it was clear than RJ was one of a number of approaches used to respond to conflict and problem behaviour. Other measures existed alongside RJ, leading to responses that were not restorative. As one manager said:

> '[There are] still too many consequences, too many "early beds"…. What's the point? How does it relate to what's going on most of the time?'

In both periods of fieldwork, some care staff reported relatively limited perceived options for what could be done in terms of reparation. Typically, care staff listed possibilities such as cleaning up, apologising, shaking hands and paying towards the replacement of something broken, although this was rare because of the prohibitive cost. In some homes, there were examples of young people writing letters of apology, and in one case, reparation was very much part of the incentive scheme developed by the home. In cases where RJ was combined with an incentive scheme, staff reported that problems and conflicts were dealt with satisfactorily early on.

As noted above, a minority of staff felt frustrated or negative about the usefulness of RJ when young people failed to change their behaviour after an RJ meeting. Some staff appeared to have unrealistic expectations about what RJ might achieve with children and young people in care. In some cases, these staff may have lacked insight into how their own behaviour needed to change. These problems were acknowledged by other members of staff, typically those who were supporters of the approach. For example, as one of the RJ coordinators said:

'The process is the reparation. We can't look for change in behaviour or attitude.'

He went on to say that he felt RJ 'encouraged the development of emotional literacy' and recognised that any change or development had to be seen as a long-term process with children and young people. Some staff did not appreciate this viewpoint and wanted to see more immediate changes in young people's behaviour if they were going to be persuaded that RJ was a worthwhile approach.

Training

One of the key aspects of the initial three-day training was the focus on scripted conferences.

Some staff felt uncomfortable with the idea of being responsible for setting up a conference. In one unit, this had resulted in one person taking on the role of setting up and running conferences. The other staff came to rely on this individual such that if they wanted to hold a conference they would have to wait until he was on shift and had time to set one up. Most homes, however, quickly adopted a more informal approach. The following quotes (2006 fieldwork) about the initial training and formal use of RJ were common:

'Nothing [in the training] encouraged its informal use.'

'The formal approach is artificial in a home environment.'

'The principles are fantastic but need applying to the more specific needs of the situation and client group in residential care – as happens with Team-Teach.'

One period of training was felt to be insufficient, and further comparison was made with the already well-established Team-Teach approach, which was thought to be more adaptable: "It's flexible, with annual updates for all staff." Staff explained how the Team-Teach approach was more interactive; in one case, for example, Team-

Teach had changed aspects of their positive handling strategies as a result of feedback from staff.

Follow-up RJ training took place in early 2007, involving managers and (mainly) RJ coordinators from each home. This time, the training focused on more informal uses of RJ, referred to as 'street RJ' by the trainers (staff sometimes used the terms 'corridor RJ' or 'stand-up RJ' instead). The refresher training was generally well received. One manager said, "We came back quite inspired," while an RJ coordinator commented, "The refresher training showed that it's not all about conferences."

However, a common view was that refresher training was needed for all staff, not just managers and RJ coordinators:

> 'Refresher training for all staff, not just RJ coordinators. Greater emphasis put on RJ recording, especially after an incident.... Greater emphasis on using RJ to resolve social conflict not just criminal activities.'

> '[We need] proper training – if we are going to do this thing properly, we need more than the course I went on two years ago; that wasn't specific to our home.'

The need for the training to be extended to others involved with children in care was also raised:

> '[We need a] more rounded approach to training which includes education, social workers, foster carers.'

Indeed, the original aspiration of the local authority was that other professionals working with children and young people would embrace the RJ approach. Certainly, the YOT was using RJ, but in a more formal conferencing style (and supported by a different training organisation), and there were no resources to extend training to foster carers, field social workers or indeed teachers. Herein lies one of the problems with approaches like RJ that often rely on the work of specialist organisations training relatively small groups of people at costs that may not be available in all training budgets. Whether other professionals could be expected to understand and embrace the principles of RJ without training is an interesting question.

Reflecting on the initial training (2007 fieldwork), some staff were critical:

> 'Too formal, to a script, where you were pulled up if you didn't use the exact words.'

Others were more positive:

> 'On reflection the teaching of a conference approach was the gold standard, it was probably necessary to start with.'

In conclusion, our fieldwork showed that RJ was being used regularly and increasingly informally across all units and that staff attitudes towards, and evaluation of, the approach had moved in a positive direction in most respects. However, a minority of staff had clearly not embraced the approach and this could lead to frustration for managers and colleagues, as well as an inconsistent approach for children. The field research also points up some practice issues that need further consideration when implementing this approach in group settings such as in residential care, particularly the principle of voluntarism and RJ (there was an expectation that staff *should* adopt this approach and this meant that some pressures would be passed on to children and young people to do the same); reparation and restorative outcomes, which were an underdeveloped part of the process; and the sometimes unrealistic staff expectations of changed behaviour from young people; and the likely impact of RJ on young people. Finally, the suitability of RJ for use with all children and young people in care had not been fully considered, specifically in relation to those who had difficulties with empathy and/or special educational needs and disabilities that made meaningful participation in an RJ encounter highly problematic.

Children and young people's views

6

Introduction

This chapter focuses on 43 interviews with children and young people and the analysis of 38 short questionnaires completed during these interviews. These data were collected during the same two periods of fieldwork as the staff interviews: autumn 2006 and 2007. Short questionnaires (two sides of A4 paper) were completed either by the young people or researchers during face-to-face interviews. This approach had the advantage of enabling the researchers to explain the questions and giving young people the opportunity to expand on their answers. The questionnaires focused first on young people's perceptions of staff management of behaviour within the homes and second, on how a particular problem had been 'sorted out'. We did not assume that all young people would know what restorative justice (RJ) meant, so we focused mainly on getting a picture of how behaviour was managed by staff. We did ask two direct questions about half way through the interviews, after we had explored perceptions of how staff set boundaries and responded to the behaviour of children and young people: first, the young people were asked whether they knew what RJ meant; they were then asked to give an example of a situation where staff had been involved in 'sorting out a problem' and whether they thought the staff response to 'sorting out a problem' constituted 'restorative justice'. Questions about restorative justice were therefore asked within the broader framework of young people's perceptions of how problem behaviour and conflict was managed by staff within the residential care environment.

Researching children and young people in care

Including children and young people in research that concerns their welfare was an important principle in this study. Local authority managers were particularly keen to get young people's perspective. Some residential care staff were adamant about the right of young people to make their own decision to participate, rather than have the decision made by an adult before being approached for their consent. Heptinstall (2000) writes of the time-consuming process of gaining access to children in care as an external researcher, noting the tendency of a variety of adult 'gatekeepers' to protect children from the perceived adverse effects of participation in research. Clearly, there is 'a potential conflict between children's rights to be heard and an adult's duty to promote the children's best interests' (Heptinstall, 2000, p 872). She concludes that adult concerns about children's participation in research can prevent some children from being included in research when they want to give their view.

Barnardo's (2006) acknowledges these issues in its advice about exceptions to routinely asking for parental consent. It suggests that this may not be necessary in cases where the research is of minimal risk to the young person, where relationships may have broken down between children and their parents and, where children may not want their parents informed or involved. These issues were very pertinent to the current research in terms of ethical review of the proposal and in managing the dichotomy between local authorities' desire to get children's views and the young people's right *not* to participate. Indeed, the current research encountered relatively few barriers from adult gatekeepers, probably partly because children were in a group care setting with several care staff around when the researchers visited the homes; often a member of staff would help facilitate opportunities to talk and had already prepared the young people for our visit. In addition, young people may already have seen us around the home during other visits to collect data before we approached them for an interview. This piqued their curiosity about who we were and what we were doing. Sometimes those young people who had initially refused to be interviewed saw others taking part and subsequently decided that they also wanted to 'have their say'.

Previous experience of researching children and young people meant that it was recognised from the outset that too much focus on RJ might not be very meaningful (or interesting) to some individuals; what adults want to know is not always what children want to talk about. It was also known that literacy and concentration levels were likely to vary widely across an age group that spanned nine to 17 years and included some individuals with special educational needs. These were major considerations in relation to how we tackled this part of the study. There is a great deal of literature available on research involving children (see, for example, Harker, 2002), and this served as a useful reminder of the additional ethical considerations when researching children; these issues were outlined in Chapter Two. Questions that are especially pertinent to researching children and young people in care are as follows:

- Who grants access and has parental responsibility?
- What are the limits to confidentiality?
- What are the responsibilities of the researcher in relation to what children say and what they may observe in the care setting?

These considerations make researching children and young people in care an activity that must be very carefully planned, with a clear protocol about what to do in the event of a child or young person raising child protection concerns, or in the event of a researcher raising concerns about the way a home appears to be operating.

This study had the advantage that one of the researchers has long experience in researching children and the other had trained as a social worker. We also had trusted professionals who had agreed to act as the first port of call in case of an issue arising during fieldwork. Furthermore, we were able to develop our data collection methods in consultation with care staff working in homes. After consultation with staff, it was decided that two questionnaires were needed – one with 'smiley faces' (see Table 6.1) and one that looked like the staff questionnaire, with statements and numbers on a Likert scale (as it was thought that some of the older teenagers may take exception to the more childish appearance of the 'smiley faces' questionnaire). In practice, the judgement about which questionnaire was used in a particular setting was not based simply on the age group of the interviewees, although the smiley faces questionnaire was always used with the younger children in the 2006 interviews and in the end only eight young people completed the adult-style questionnaire. By the second round of interviews in autumn 2007, it was decided to use only the smiley faces questionnaire, part of which is replicated in Table 6.1. It became clear that young people did not have a problem with this style of questionnaire, with some recognising the type of format as being similar to that of the incident-recording forms used in the home. We therefore reassigned the responses from the eight adult-style questionnaires (from autumn 2006) so that all responses could be reported in the same format (see Figure 6.1).

A key issue in conducting research with these young people was flexibility, both in terms of how the questionnaire was used, and how, where and when young people were encouraged to talk. This meant that in some cases interviews were held outside the unit, in the grounds of the home, for example, while the interviewee had a cigarette, and on another occasion the young person agreed to complete the questionnaire in exchange for help with their homework. A few young people (see below) were suspicious about completing a questionnaire but were willing to talk. We wanted to talk to young people individually but in a few cases we talked to them in a pair or in one case in a group of three. It was important to make the experience as enjoyable as possible for the young people, to take what they said seriously and to show interest in what they had to say. The great majority seemed to enjoy having their say and being the subject of adult interest and attention. Although the young people were given no incentive to participate in advance, they received a £20 HMV voucher as a 'thank you' for their time once all the interviews in a home were completed. In the spirit of the whole RJ venture, the voucher was for all residents in the home, with most staff saying they would accompany individuals to spend the voucher when they had decided what they wanted as a group.

Interviews with young people were undertaken in nine of the 10 residential homes in autumn 2006 and in six of the eight homes in autumn 2007. The main reasons for not interviewing young people were that they were not available at the time of the visit or that they refused to take part. Over the two periods of field research, a total of 43 children were interviewed, 38 of whom were also willing to complete questionnaires. It should be noted when interpreting these findings that it is likely that the research *underrepresents* the views of children and young people who were the *least amenable*, either because they were not in the home at the times the researchers visited, or were unwilling to take part.

Perceptions of staff management of behaviour

As Table 6.1 illustrates, 38 young people completed questionnaires (21 in autumn 2006 and 17 in autumn 2007). Fewer young people were consulted in the second round of fieldwork for a number of reasons: fewer homes were open, as already noted, or fewer young people were available for interview in some homes (either because there were fewer residents in total or because young people were 'missing', 'unauthorised absent' or not in the home on the day of the visit for another reason). Nevertheless, it is estimated that around half the young people officially resident (if not actually available on the day of interview) were consulted during the visits to homes.

Table 6.1: Young people's views (2006, 2007)

Statement	Yes	Not sure	No
I know how staff expect me to behave here	35 (92.1%)	3	–
The rules here are clear	25 (65.8%)	7	6
Staff are fair when I am being difficult	23 (60.5%)	14	1
Staff are fair when other young people are being difficult	26 (68.4%)	10	2
Staff talk things through with me when there is a problem	32 (84.2%)	4	2
I know that staff will help me if other young people are upsetting me	33 (86.8%)	5	–
I know what 'restorative justice' means	16 (42.1%)	11	11

N = 38

Table 6.1 shows that the strongest level of agreement is for 'I know how staff expect me to behave', 'I know that staff will help me if other young people are upsetting me' and 'Staff talk things through with me when there is a problem'. The young people were divided about whether they knew what RJ meant: only 16 of the 38 young people interviewed immediately agreed with the statement 'I know what "restorative justice" means', with the rest evenly divided between 'not sure' and not knowing what it meant. However, once the researcher had explained the basic principles, some of the young people understood what it was and were able to explain it back to the interviewer, or showed intuitive understanding of it in the examples they gave about how a problem was 'sorted out'.

Comparing responses in 2006 and 2007

Despite a smaller sample from fewer units in the second period of fieldwork (six units in 2007, compared with nine in 2006), Figure 6.1 shows a strong similarity in much of the overall pattern of response between the two time periods. In particular, statements about staff expectations of behaviour and knowing that staff would help if they were upset had an even higher rating in the second period of field research. The latter finding is important in relation to what we know from child abuse enquiries (for example, Waterhouse et al, 2000), and suggests that the majority of young people interviewed had an adult they felt they could go to if they were in difficulty. Having an adult to go to is seen as key to preventing problems and abuse in care.

The main areas of change between 2006 and 2007 were in young people's perception of whether the rules are clear (2006, 73%; 2007, 53%) and in relation to staff fairness when they were being difficult where there was conflict (2006, 64%; 2007, 53%). This shift appears to relate to a major change in the dynamics within one home during the period of fieldwork and is, of course, influenced by the relatively small number of children involved in this part of the research. The latter finding also reflects the

Figure 6.1: Comparing young people's views (2006, 2007)

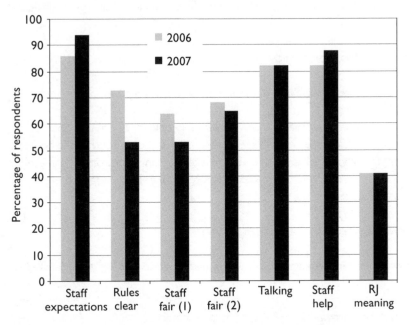

Notes: Staff expectations = 'I know how staff expect me to behave here'; Rules clear = 'The rules here are clear'; Staff fair (1) = 'Staff are fair when *I* am being difficult'; Staff fair (2) = 'Staff are fair when *other* young people are being difficult'; Talking = 'Staff talk things through with me when there is a problem'; Staff help = 'I know that staff will help me if other young people are upsetting me'; RJ meaning = 'I know what "restorative justice" means'.

2006, N= 22 completed questionnaires and 4 interviews; 2007, N = 17 completed questionnaires differences apparent within staff groups (in the autumn 2007 interviews) in relation to whether they supported the RJ approach, as noted in Chapter Five.

What do young people think 'restorative justice' means?

Both sets of field research found that some young people felt that they knew and understood what the RJ approach was and were confident enough to say what they thought it meant. Quotes from young people emphasised communication and feelings, as the following examples show:

> 'What you think you've done, what you were feeling at the time.' (Male, age 11)

> 'Get a chance to have your say, what these questions are all about.' (Male, age 14)

> 'Talking things through.' (Female, age 16)

Two teenagers who were interviewed in both 2006 and 2007 had little understanding of RJ in 2006 but felt they did understand it when interviewed in 2007. One emphasised the key issue of taking responsibility:

> 'It's where we have to take responsibility for our behaviour and say sorry.' (Male, aged 14)

The other focused on communication:

> 'It's where we have to talk about what we've done.' (Male, aged 14)

Furthermore, in other comments made by young people, a change was apparent in the way their home was operating. In 2006, they said that the approach in the home to dealing with conflict was to apply sanctions, which often involved 'loss of' something. In 2007, the same young people made reference to restorative approaches, rather than to 'loss of' approaches.

Some individuals in effect talked about 'reparation':

> 'If you do something wrong, staff give you something positive to do.' (Female, aged 15)

Others saw what followed an RJ meeting as 'punishment':

> 'Meetings to do with behaviour, to decide on the punishment.' (Female, age 13)

Still other focused on understanding their own behaviour, how it affected other people (perhaps reflecting something approaching empathy) and how it taught them to keep out of trouble another time:

'It is about reflecting on our behaviour.' (Male, aged 12)

'We have to answer some questions about how we feel, what we were doing, what we were thinking, (how) next time I will not get involved.' (Male, aged 12)

'We talk about what has happened and how to stop it next time.' (Male, aged 13)

'Talk about your behaviour, how it affects other people and what you can do to be better.' (Female, aged 13)

A quote that local authority social services managers particularly liked was:

'The way things are done here.' (Female, age 13)

This implied that staff had achieved a consistent (or at least clear) approach in some homes.

Overall, although initial responses to the questionnaire appear to show a limited understanding of the formal concept of 'restorative justice'; it became apparent, when talking to young people about a specific situation or event, that they could identify key aspects of the practice in the way in which a situation was resolved.

Examples of 'sorting out problems'

Young people were asked to provide an example of how a recent problem had been 'sorted out'. Most young people were able to do so, with some illustrating that a restorative approach had been used. Respondents mainly cited relatively minor altercations when asked to give an example of the last time they had a problem with another young person; examples included teasing or turning off the computer when somebody was using it. The young people, however, could get very wound up about this sort of thing and often felt that such incidents should be sorted out by staff. Another example might be swearing and abusive language. As one young person said about such an incident:

'Staff should find out what happened to make him swear.'(Male, age 12)

A particularly interesting example of a problem that was perceived to be more serious was given by an 11-year-old boy who said he had spent about four days building a Lego castle that was then kicked over by another young person. In this case, the person who had kicked over the castle was sent to bed early. The boy who built the castle was unhappy about this and thought that there should have been an RJ meeting – he wanted help to rebuild his castle. Although this boy said he did not know what RJ meant, he demonstrates an intuitive understanding of the principles in the example he gave of a problem and his desired resolution (or reparation).

Fighting and bullying behaviour featured in other examples given:

> 'As me and [A] had a fight a couple of days ago we had to answer some questions about what we were doing, how we were feeling and what we would do next time.' (Male, aged 11)

> 'We were winding each other up and bullying other children. Staff said that we had to sort it out so we sat at a table and talked about how we were going to get on with each other.' (Male, aged 11)

Both young people were happy with what happened after the event they described and thought that what was done was an example of restorative justice.

In other cases, there was limited or no evidence of a restorative approach being taken. For example, one young person who said that he had never heard of RJ described a situation in the following way:

> 'They were talking about my sister. Two people started this. I told staff. They got grounded for 48 hours.' (Male, aged 12)

The response was clearly based on a sanction. However, when the young person was asked whether he was happy about it, he said, "Yes ... because it worked!".

Some young people chose to focus on conflicts with staff, as the following two examples show. In one example, the issue was ongoing and involved a young woman (15 years old), who, by her own admission, was in conflict with staff:

> 'The problem was that I had an argument with staff and was abusive. I started it.'

When asked how often kind of thing happened, she replied, "Every day"; she realised that she became abusive very quickly. She described the staff response to the last time this had happened as follows:

> 'I was sat down and spoken to and told that if I have a problem, then speak to staff.'

This young person said she was happy with what was done in this situation and that she thought that what was done was an example of restorative justice. Another incident illustrated a more serious conflict between young people. Again, the respondent was a young woman (13 years old):

'I'd been the victim in a fight [and was] moved to respite [foster family] until the perpetrator moved on…. The police were called and needed to break the door down … she was prosecuted and [I] never saw her again.'

The young person was 'happy' that the perpetrator was prosecuted but 'didn't know' whether or not this was an example of restorative justice.

Three young people mentioned wanting to have the police called over an event involving another young person, although two of them went on to say that they were glad that this *was not* the outcome, because they were now friends with the young person with whom they had been in conflict. This illustrates the difficult decisions staff have to make in response to an incident between young people, as well as the potential for unintended consequences if staff understanding of the right of young people to have police involvement is acted on too quickly or 'in the heat of the moment'.

Managing behaviour and the residential care environment

In autumn 2006, five young people interviewed in two homes (two in one home, three in the other) did not want to complete a questionnaire, although they were willing to respond to some general questions. One of the interesting aspects to these interviews was the insights they offered on the residential environment. For example, in reply to the question, 'What would make the home a better place to live in?', one young man identified a more equal gender mix (a theme that emerges elsewhere in the following section). When asked why he held this view, he replied that he wanted to see a move away from the 'macho' behaviour he felt was exhibited in the home. The gender mix was seen as a source of conflict in other homes. Two female respondents said that in their home they were no longer able to sit in the same room as a male resident from whom they were subject to 'horrible' comments about themselves and their families. Bullying behaviour was also mentioned (unsolicited) in this home. One young person commented:

'If one person is a bully then they should be moved on.'

Staff not listening was identified as an issue in both the homes where children declined to complete questionnaires in 2006. As one young person said:

'Staff need to listen to us. Listen as we need help.'

Another commented:

'[Staff] need more discussion with young people.'

In relation to not being listened to, one young woman gave an example of finding it difficult to get to sleep and feeling frightened at night. In the past she had had carers who increased the amount of time she was left alone at night before going to check on her. She had asked for the same support in the home she was in at the time of interview, but reported that only one member of staff would respond to this request. She said that:

> 'The rest say they will return but never do.'

In interviews with young people in two other units (where young people did complete questionnaires), other important comments were made about the management of behaviour and the care environment. These comments were made while the young people were completing the questionnaires and in response to the questions asked there. In one interview, the subject of the use of restraint and sanctions came up very quickly. The young person said:

> 'Staff use sanctions really quickly.'

Another in the same unit said:

> 'Staff use restraint straight away with me, with no warning.'

Both young people also felt that they 'started' on people themselves very quickly, verbally in the first case and physically in the second case. In the case where restraint was reported, the young person said that this happened every few days and related to her attacking another young woman as soon as she was in the same room. The reason for the attacks was said to be comments that this young woman had made about a member of her family, based on information overheard when care staff were talking about the young person.

Another young person confirmed the use of sanctions:

> 'They [the staff] switch off the electricity all the time.'

Sanctions mentioned in other interviews included 'supervised spending of pocket money', which prevented young people from purchasing alcohol or cigarettes. Two young women said that staff often called the police in response to conflict. These young women believed that staff could be more lenient with the male residents, claiming that "boys seem to get away with it", although they couldn't elaborate further on this view. One of these young women said she had identified a new tendency for staff to start to walk away from young people who were in conflict rather than to listen to them. These two young people could not identify any consequences for problem behaviour other than sanctions and said that they could not identify any restorative outcomes within the home. However, one of these young women demonstrated that they understood the concept of restorative justice as "paying back to society", connecting this to the fact that she was subject to a referral order. She said that at some point in the future she had to write a letter of apology to her friend after being involved in a burglary at her bed-sit. She had not experienced or observed anything similar to this in the way problem behaviour was tackled in the home.

In another home, two young women wanted to emphasise the problems they perceived as arising from the mix of young people in the unit. Although this was a short-term unit, one of the young women had lived there for around a year. For her, "boys are the problem":

> 'I prefer the staff, they're not twats, some of the kids are mad.... They should know more about the kid before they put them here. It's scary sometimes because you don't know what they'll do.'

A couple of weeks before the interview, the young woman had been locked in the staff office with members of staff and another young woman, waiting for the police to come while a young man smashed the windows and shouted threats at them (an incident referred to in Chapter Four). The young woman was adamant that the police should have been called in:

> '[The] police should be called, somebody could get hurt, nobody knew [the young man involved].'

Independently, a young woman in the same home said in a private interview (with reference to the same event):

> '... people like that shouldn't be in this sort of care, they should be in secure.'

Staff inconsistency was highlighted both in the questionnaires and in relation to what young people said, with one person (who was unwilling to complete a questionnaire) characterising the differences in staff response to conflict in the following way:

> 'It depends. One member of staff goes into the office and starts crying, another starts shouting and swearing, one takes the piss and another lets us get on with it.'

As with staff, the overall picture presented in the interviews with children and young people was fairly complex and inevitably related in part to the specific context of the homes in which they were resident at the time of interview and questionnaire completion. For example, in several homes, it was clear that individual young people had ongoing conflicts with other residents. 'Sanctions' as a concept was well understood by all young people, although some did not immediately understand the concept of 'restorative justice' (evident in their response to a direct question or to questions relating to staff response to a particular problem). Nevertheless, most young people indicated that they knew how staff expected them to behave and that the rules were clear. They also showed some awareness that they could be the ones to initiate conflicts with other young people, but usually felt that this was justified. The young people often claimed that individual staff responded to problematic behaviour differently. Most of the young people completing questionnaires thought that staff would help them if another young person were upsetting them. A more negative picture came from the five young people (from two homes) who were unwilling to complete questionnaires but did talk to the researcher visiting in the 2006 fieldwork. Furthermore, another four young people (in two different homes) who talked in more depth while completing their questionnaires in 2006 raised some important and problematic issues about the management of volatile behaviour in the residential environment. These interviews with young people make for uncomfortable reading. They confirm the finding in the staff interviews that an RJ approach was not embraced by all care staff. They also remind us of the difficulties of implementing a change such as restorative justice in a way that is meaningful to children and young people.

What happens during a period of residential care?

7

Introduction

This chapter takes a closer look at individual children and what happens to them during a period of residential care, specifically in relation to problematic or offending behaviour. The evidence draws on two sources: a one-year cohort study starting with all children resident or admitted to children's residential care in a one-month period in 2006 (46 children in all) and case studies of 16 children through an analysis of case file data (and follow-up on information gaps with care staff where necessary) during the summer of 2007. Both these sources of data relied heavily on the support of local authority staff. The cohort study was set up and based on existing data collected on the children within social care and cross-referenced (for accuracy and additional information) with education and youth offending team staff. The case file data collection was undertaken by care staff, following consultation and training. Staff visited a children's home other than their own to collate data on two children (one who had arrived with a record of offending behaviour and one who had no such record). The cohort study illustrates the extent to which a group of children get into trouble (if at all) during a period of residential care. This part of the research tracked any offending behaviour in the context of the nature and duration of the care experience, alongside evidence about educational participation. The case studies investigated in more depth the kind of behaviours presented at the level of the home (including offending behaviour); whether there was any evidence of a restorative justice (RJ) approach being used with an individual and what impact, if any, it had; and, an overall assessment of key aspects of the current residential care episode on individual children.

In Chapter Two, we took a critical look at the notion of 'outcomes' and care and the extent to which outcomes can be ascribed to the care experience. One of the difficulties is in ascertaining whether any problems that arise are linked to living in care or to what happens to children and young people before they enter the care system. We also highlighted that outcomes are usually presented in relation to all children in care, with no distinctions made between residential and other forms of care. This chapter addresses the latter issue, as all children in this study are in residential care. The former issue is more complex, although we refer to information on the backgrounds of children and their circumstances of entry into care within the case studies. We have used staff assessments of the impact of care in the 16 case studies. We have chosen the term 'what happens', rather than outcomes, in order to raise the question of whether the care experience is necessarily the main explanation of conflicts and offending behaviour.

The cohort study

The cohort for this study comprises 46 children and young people who were already resident or admitted into the 10 children's homes open in November 2006. The number was a little lower than expected because most of the young people in the secure unit at that time were not from the local authority (and we did not have permission to include children outside the local authority in our study). In addition, some homes had only four or five residents at the time the study was set up and there was only one emergency placement in that month. The characteristics of the cohort are outlined below.

Characteristics of the cohort

The key characteristics of the group are as follows:

Gender: 29 (63%) male, 17 (37%) female

Age: mean 14.6 years at the *end* of the cohort year (range 10-17 years)

Ethnicity: not recorded on the database

Time in care (at the *end* of the cohort year): looked after child (LAC) *less than* a year: 14 (30.4%); LAC *more than* a year: 32 (69.6%)

Movements in care: the majority of those in care during the year (41, 89.1%) were cared for continuously; five individuals moved out of care and returned; around a third (16, 34.8%) were no longer looked after at the end of the cohort year

The cohort was a relatively stable group, with around three quarters (35, 76%) being placed in the same home throughout the time they were looked after during the year. Only two individuals had three placements (all in residential care) during the year. The rest either had two placements (again, both in residential care) or left care during the year. At the start of the year, around six in 10 placements (27, 59%) were described as 'long term' and nearly a quarter (11, 24%) were 'short term', the rest included remands (two), place of safety (two), emergency placements (one) and 'other' (three) placements. This illustrates more stability of placement than would be found across all children in care in this local authority, illustrating that, for many children, residential care was (as several staff said) 'the end of the line.'

Offending

By the end of the one-year period, around two thirds of the children and young people (30, 65.2%) had an official record of offending *during the cohort year*. A further five young people had an official record of offending outside the cohort year. Therefore, in total around three quarters (35, 76.1%) of the cohort group had a record of offending behaviour. Overall, the mean number of offences for those offending in the cohort year was 4.7, with a range of one to 16 offences.

Figure 7.1: Cohort study: percentage of young people who had a record of offending

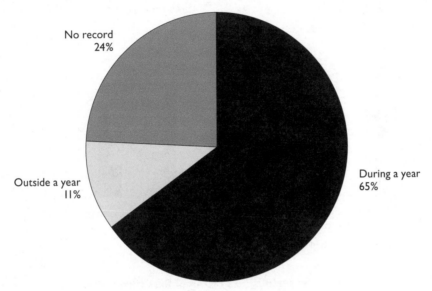

No record
24%

Outside a year
11%

During a year
65%

N = 46

As the number and range of offences recorded against individuals is quite complex, we have focused on the first three offences and the most common categories of offence in Figure 7.2. The categories are those used within the criminal justice system. Figure 7.2 shows that 'violence against the person' is the most common type of offence. Nearly half of the cohort (22, 47.8%) had such a record. Less frequently recorded offences were burglary (three records across offence 1 and 2) and vehicle theft/unauthorised taking (four records across offences 2 and 3).

Offences are also rated by seriousness (from 1-8, with 8 being the most serious type of offence, that is, murder, and 1 including offences such as rail fare evasion or being drunk and disorderly). These ratings are based on the way the Youth Justice Board rates the seriousness of a crime (see YJB, 2009). Table 7.1 shows the seriousness of offending across the first three offences and the most serious offence. The most serious offence is the one that has the highest rating from 1-8. We do not have data on the type and seriousness of offence for three of the 35 individuals in the cohort who have offended. The most serious offences within this cohort included attempted robbery or attempted burglary (rated 6) and false imprisonment (rated 7).

Figure 7.2: Cohort study: most common types of offence (first three offences)

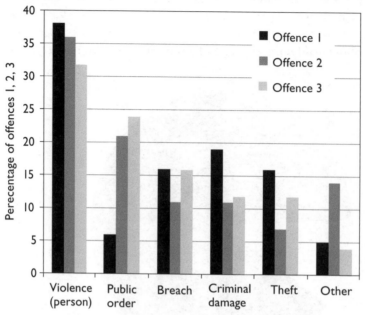

N = 32 of 35 with a record of offending; details unclear in three cases.

Table 7.1: Cohort study: seriousness rating of first three offences

Seriousness rating 1-8	Offence 1 Number (%)	Offence 2 Number (%)	Offence 3 Number (%)	Most serious offence
1	2 (6.3%)	1 (3.6%)	2 (8%)	–
2	8 (25%)	10 (35.7%)	10 (40%)	2 (6.3%)
3	16 (50%)	12 (42.9%)	9 (36%)	14 (43.8%)
4	5 (15.6%)	3 (10.7%)	3 (12%)	9 (28.1%)
5	–	1 (3.6%)	–	3 (9.4%)
6	1 (3.1%)	1 (3.6%)	–	3 (9.4%)
7	–	–	1 (4%)	1 (3.1%)
Mean seriousness rating	2.88	2.86	2.72	3.81
Number offending	32*	28	25	32

N = 32 of 35 with a record of offending. It was not possible to obtain accurate details of the offences and seriousness in three cases.

Figure 7.3 shows the first and most serious outcome from offences known to have been committed by the young people in the cohort study. These outcomes are known as 'disposals' within the criminal justice system. The least serious disposal does not involve the court and may be a police reprimand or a final warning. Other disposals involve the courts and become progressively more severe, ending in custody (see www.yjb.gov.uk for further information about how aspects of the system work). Figure 7.3 illustrates a move towards more serious disposals between the first outcome recorded and the most serious outcome: with seven young people in custody at the end of the cohort year, compared with two at the start of the year.

Figure 7.3: Cohort study: disposals for the first and most serious recorded offence

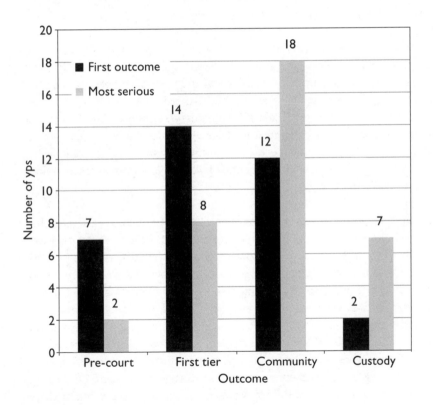

Notes:

Pre-court = police reprimand, final warnings.

First-tier = various orders, eg referral order, fine, conditional discharge.

Community = various orders, eg attendance centre, curfew, supervision.

Custody = detention and training order, sections 90/91, 226 and 228 (note no young people detained for the latter sections in this sample).

N = 35

Education

Attendance in mainstream education is how most young people obtain their GCSE and equivalent qualifications at the age of 16. An investigation of how children and young people in residential care are educated reveals that mainstream educational participation is uncommon. We tracked educational provision across the year at four points, autumn 2006, spring 2007, summer 2007 and autumn 2007 (see Figure 7.4). These data show that at most 14 of the 46 young people (30.4%) attended mainstream education facilities, with education in pupil referral units (PRUs) and outside a mainstream or special school being the most common type of provision. In other words, at the start of the one-year cohort study (autumn 2006), more young people were attending a PRU or similar provision than a mainstream school (18, 39.1%). Indeed, taken together, those attending a PRU or similar provision, a special school or secure accommodation made up over half (25, 54.3%) of the young people at the start of this part of the research.

A minority of young people (three) were not of compulsory school age at the start of the cohort year, with a bigger group (13) falling into this category by the end. Four individuals had no educational provision at the start of the cohort year: two were aged 15 at the time and had no recorded provision until they reached school leaving age; two were younger (11 and 13 years) but were soon in education (one in a mainstream school and one in a special school). Educational provision changed for one in five young people during the year (nine, 19.6%). Ten young people in all had left care by the end of the year and all but one of these (a young boy in special school) were 16 or nearly 16.

Exclusion from school is a useful indicator of problematic behaviour in a setting other than a children's home. Exclusion from school and poor attendance are also well-known 'risk factors' for offending behaviour. Over a third (17, 37%) of the cohort had a record of exclusion from school during the cohort year. This was a fixed-period exclusion in all but one case. Monitoring data from the Department for Children, Schools and Families on fixed-period exclusions in the whole school population indicate that around 2-3% might expect a fixed-period exclusion during a school year (DCSF, 2009c). Eleven of the 17 young people had more than one fixed-period exclusion. In nine cases, exclusion was not possible (not applicable or N/A in Figure 7.5), as the young person was either not of compulsory school age (in the case of three individuals at the start of the cohort year), or was in secure accommodation (two at the start of the cohort year) or without provision (four at the start of the cohort year). The number in these latter categories changed over the cohort year. Full school attendance data for the cohort year were not available on about half the young people in the cohort, partly because these data are not collected when young people spend time outside the care system and partly because the information had not been recorded.

Figure 7.4: Cohort study: educational provision during the cohort year

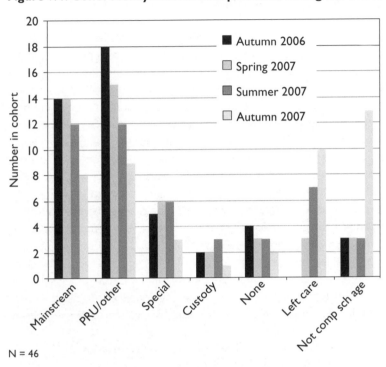

N = 46

Figure 7.5: Cohort study: whether young people had an official record of exclusion during the cohort year

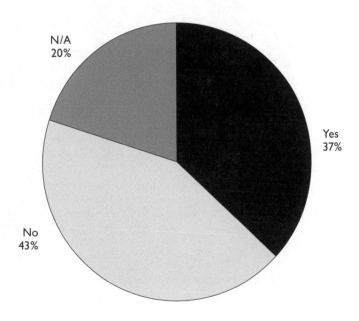

N = 46

Comparing 'offenders' and 'non-offenders'

Given the high prevalence of offending in the cohort, it became pertinent to investigate the circumstances of the 11 young people who had no record of offending either in the cohort year or before. Comparison between non-offenders and offenders showed that non-offenders' mean age was lower (13.3 years, compared with 15.1 years). Five of these 11 young people were placed in long-term homes for younger children. A further two young people were in secure accommodation for welfare reasons (and had no record of offending). Being in care was continuous for all 11 young people (that is, none went in and out of care during the year), although one of the young people left care halfway through the cohort year. However, at least two of the young people had a change of home during the year and the first placement of another two was not recorded (so it is unclear whether or not they changed homes). Seven of the 11 young people had been looked after for more than a year. Ten of the 11 young people were of compulsory school age and all 10 had educational provision. There was no change in educational provision for any of these young people during the cohort year. One young person moved from mainstream education to a PRU when they became resident in a children's home. Four young people experienced a fixed-period exclusion from school, with two of the latter having records of fixed-period

Table 7.2: Cohort study: comparison of the key characteristics and circumstances of offenders and non-offenders

	Non-offenders (N = 11)	Offenders (N = 35)
Age	13.3 years	15.1 years
Gender	M = 9 (81.8%) F = 2 (18.2%)	M = 20 (57.1%) F = 15 (42.9%)
Whether care continuous in cohort year	Yes = 11 (100%)	Yes = 30 (85.7%) No = 5 (14.3%)
Whether had educational placement, if of school age	Yes = 10 (100%) One case, not of school age	Yes = 29 (82.8%) No* = 6 (17.2%) *4 none; 2 not comp school age
Any change in educational placement during cohort year	Yes = 1 (10%) No = 9 (90%) Not applicable in one case, not of school age	Yes = 8 (22.9%) No = 23 (77.1%) Not applicable in four cases – not of school age (two), no school during year (two)
Any exclusions	Yes = 4 (40%) No = 6 (60%) Not applicable in one case, not of school age	Yes = 13 (44.8%) No = 16 (55.2%) Not applicable in six cases, four above school leaving age and two in secure accommodation (education provided on site)

Notes: * Not applicable for 2 yps who were above school leaving age.

N = 46

exclusion in more than one term. One young person had a permanent exclusion in the school term before he left the care system.

Bearing in mind that the numbers in the 'offender' and 'non offender' groups are small, Table 7.2 shows that the group who have no record of offending were generally younger and more stable in their home and educational placements in comparison with the offending group.

Case studies

By the time this part of the research was under way, two of the homes were closed, so we only had eight possible homes to cover. In the event, we were able to access seven of the eight homes (one secure, six open) and 16 young people. As the secure unit operated as two units, four case studies were undertaken in this setting (two in each home). Staff were asked to choose young people who had been resident for at least three months in the home, so that there was some time for any changes or incidents to occur (this happened in all but one case). Further, staff investigating children in the seven open units were asked to choose one individual whose offending behaviour was already known at admission and one individual where there was no such evidence. The characteristics of this sample are outlined below.

Characteristics of the sample

The key characteristics of the group are as follows:

Gender: 14 male, two female

Age: mean 13.8 years (range 11-17 years)

Ethnicity: 13 White, 3 Black and Minority Ethnic

Time resident in home: mean 42.8 weeks (range eight to 112 weeks)

As the numbers are small in this part of the research, we will present evidence by number, rather than percentage.

Entry into residential care

The reasons why these 16 young people were in residential care were varied and often complex; it is easy to see why they could be angry and aggressive. For example, a 16-year-old male came into residential care as a result of a remand following an assault on his mother. He had been on the child protection register for emotional and physical abuse and had been the carer for his two younger siblings. His mother went into a 'detox' facility for her substance misuse problems while he was in the home and his siblings were cared for by the maternal grandparents. A social worker made the following comment on this case:

> 'As there was no alternative [to residential care] it appears that there was an escalation of negative behaviour and offending behaviour during a period when applications to independent living projects were rejecting his applications. He has recently settled into residential care in the knowledge that he would be moving on to independent living.'

So at the age of 16 or 17, following all the upset and disruption in his background, the plan was for this young man to live independently in supported lodgings. Yet he was also assessed as 'high risk' because of his behaviour: he had shown violence towards staff and had been charged with actual bodily harm twice; he had gone missing or was 'unauthorised absent' several times; and he was not attending his college placement (partly because of the uncertainties about where he would be living). This case illustrates the difficulty inherent in finding an appropriate way of caring for a young man with several problematic types of behaviour and why he presents a risk both to himself and others. Independent living at the age of 16 or 17 is now very unusual for young people outside the care system, and would be extremely difficult for even the most well-adjusted, well-motivated and high-achieving young person. For such a vulnerable young person as this young man, such 'independence' is likely to spell disaster. In this context, it is interesting to reflect on the practice of comparing the outcomes of children in care with 'all children' when their circumstances are so very different.

In several cases, the end of a foster placement precipitated the move into residential care. For example, an 11-year-old boy had previously been living with his grandparents for some time because his mother had 'severe mental health issues'. His grandparents struggled to cope with his behaviour and he had physically abused his grandfather and damaged the home before being admitted to foster care. When he was moved to residential care, it was said that:

> '[He] had one previous placement in foster care which broke down due to violence towards the foster carer.…. [He was] heavily involved with police before placement."

In another case, a boy had been adopted at the age of four. His adoption broke down and he was placed in foster care. At the age of 12, after four foster placements, he went into residential care. Behavioural problems were the main reason noted for these placement breakdowns:

> '[His] adoption broke down due to behavioural difficulties after the adoptive parents had a child of their own. He was placed in four separate foster placements,

which again ended due to behavioural difficulties. He still has regular contact with his adoptive parents, which includes overnight stays with a view to moving back home permanently.... Whilst in this placement [residential care] there are weekly recordings of the young person having to be held due to assaulting staff, bullying the other young people and damaging the property.... Whilst I was at the home this young person was being told by his social worker that he would be moving to another home that was a long-term placement with older children living there.'

The young people in secure accommodation had been involved in more serious and persistent offending behaviour. For example a 14-year-old male was said to be:

'... caught up in gang culture ... has a history of offending behaviour and has been in secure accommodation [twice] before ... accommodated this time for throwing a brick at a member of the public ... this young person has a very vague past and his basic identity is not really known. A basic fact like [his] real age is an unknown ... his name was a source of doubt as well.'

It was likely that this individual was a refugee or asylum seeker, but even this was not clear. Sadly, these kinds of stories are common when researching the circumstances of children coming into care. As noted in Chapter Two, an additional feature of these children's lives is material deprivation and poverty. Added to this is the stress of coming into a residential care environment where young people have to share their living space with others who have a range of similar (and different) problems.

Police involvement and offending during residence

Three quarters (nine) of the 12 young people in open units were involved in incidents during their residence that required police intervention. The four main reasons for police involvement in these open units were: unauthorised absence (six) or 'mispers'(children notified as missing – eight); offending behaviour (eight); and behavioural problems in the home or relating to a particular incident (seven). Seven of the eight young people with a record of 'mispers' also had a record of offending behaviour.

Four of the 16 case studies involved young people resident in the secure children's home and in all of these cases young people had offended and could not offend in the community while in secure accommodation. In total, 10 of the 16 cases (four in secure homes and six in open homes) involved children with a clear record of offending prior to admission to residential care. It follows that in six cases there was no record of offending when the young person was admitted to care.

Table 7.3 shows that five of the six young people who arrived at an open home with a record of offending also went on to offend during their residence in the home; three of the six who had no record of offending on arrival had a record of offending while resident in a home.

Table 7.3: Case studies: offending during residence, compared with offending at admission

Whether an offender at admission	Whether offended during residence in home			Total
	Yes	No	In secure home	
Yes	5	1	4	10
No	3	3	0	6
Total	8	4	4	16

N = 16

Some individuals appeared to offend more frequently during their time in care. For example, a 14-year-old male who had a previous conviction (described as 'minor') before being admitted into care had a record of criminal behaviour in five of the seven months after coming into care. During this time, he was involved in incidents of criminal damage to the children's home on several occasions and was charged with assault, disorderly behaviour, taking without owner's consent, theft and finally burglary. At this point, he was bailed to the home with a curfew and tag. He had also been excluded from school for assault and aggressive behaviour. A consideration for staff trying to understand how offending could escalate in this way was the extent to which alcohol and drugs were involved. As one member of staff commented:

> 'It is not clear how much his alcohol and substance misuse is escalating parallel to his disengagement with the service.'

Young people who did not offend

As in the cohort study, we were interested in understanding why some children did not offend while in care, particularly when it became clear that offending was more common than not offending. In all, four of the 12 young people in open units did not have a record of offending during their period of residence. These young people were very different, but they had a number of things in common (see Table 7.4). Three of the four did not have a record of offending at admission and the young person who did (and then did not offend further) was an 11-year-old boy in a long-term home for younger children; all aspects of his care were assessed as 'very positive'. Two of the four young people had no incident records (IRs) and the two that did had very few. None had IRs where aggression had been shown towards staff. Three of the four had no records of involvement with the police and in the case of the young person who did, the involvement related to numerous 'mispers' only. Apart from the absence of very aggressive behaviour, the other thing that all four young people had in common was full-time educational provision. Their education was described as 'very positive' (in three cases) or 'not a problem to start with' (one case).

Table 7.4: Case studies: young people who did not offend during residence

Gender, age, weeks resident	Risk	IRs?	Police involvement?	Education provision (whether SEN), whether any change	Impact of care on education	Number of RJ records, evidence of impact
Male, 17years, 52 weeks	Low	No	No	College (SEN), no change	'Very positive'	1, none
Female, 15 years, 72 weeks	High	3 (non-physical)	43 'mispers'	Provision out of school, change from mainstream	'Very positive'	7, 'OK'
Male, 15 years, 8 weeks	High	1 (property)	No	Mainstream (SEN), no change	'Not a problem to start with'	1, none
Male, 11 years, 24 weeks	Med	No	No	Special (SEN), no change	'Very positive'	5, 'very positive'

N = 4, of the 16 case studies

Incident records

We looked at the overall pattern of IRs in all homes over a seven-year period in Chapter Four, establishing that these records focus on aggressive and violent behaviour. Ten of the 16 young people were the subject of an IR during their residence in a home. Table 7.5 shows that all of the 10 young people who had a record of some type of incident had a record of 'non-physical aggression towards a person' and nine had a record of 'violence towards property'. Physical aggression was apparent in seven of the 10 cases, including violence towards staff. Physical aggression involved injury in five cases. Records of sexual and racial harassment were less common, but where they occurred tended to be associated with individuals with several IRs that included behaviour in all categories.

The third column in Table 7.5 gives some idea of the number of records for different types of incident. The range gives the lowest and highest number recorded for each type of incident for individual young people. Four of the ten individuals had multiple records in all categories, with one individual being at the highest end of the range in all but the sexual and racial categories.

Table 7.5: Case studies: young people who had an incident record and types of incident

Type of incident	Number of young people	Range in number of records per young person
Aggressive physical contact with injury	5	2-13
Aggressive physical contact without injury	7	1-99
Non-physical aggressive behaviour towards a person	10	2-80
Violence towards staff	7	1-89
Violence towards property	9	1-45
Sexual harassment	4	1-4
Racial harassment	4	1-3
All incidents/all young people	10	1-99

N = 10, of the 16 case studies

Some of the incidents could be extremely dangerous. For example, the reason for calling the police about one incident related to the individual concerned "tying a cord around a member of staff's neck. [He got a] three-month referral order (one hour per week with the YOT [youth offending team])." For others it was a case of "mainly background damage to property in/out of home".

The young person with the highest number of IRs (99 records) was a 12-year-old girl. Little was known about her other than she was on a care order and not in education when she was admitted to care. She was involved in multiple incidents of all types, including 13 instances of 'aggressive physical contact *with injury*' (emphasis added) and 89 records of 'violence towards staff'. However, the home managed to get her into full-time, mainstream education, where she went on to be excluded for five days for violence towards staff and other students.

Use of restorative justice

There was documented evidence of the use of restorative approaches in the majority of cases (13 out of 16), although a clear assessment on file of the relative success of using an RJ approach was limited to only seven cases. In these seven cases, the assessment of the relative effectiveness of using RJ was very mixed: effective (one case); OK (three cases); not effective (three cases). However, further evidence and comments from staff carrying out the case studies helped explain these results:

'The young person has been unable to engage in the restorative approach. This could be due to the young person's learning disability being diagnosed as Asperger's [experiencing the signs and symptoms of Asperger syndrome]. While there are many records of RJ being used, the impact in terms of change is not evidenced.'

Sometimes it was more a question of whether informal uses of RJ had been recorded:

'It is very clear that following this episode of care, albeit a custodial one, the young person in this study has benefited greatly from the boundaries and security of their placement. Prior to being looked after, the young person was heavily involved in crime and cannabis use and this obviously had a major impact on the course life has taken. Although there are no recorded incidents of the use of RJ, after speaking to the deputy, they assured me that RJ is being used on a "corridor-type basis". However, looking at the fact that there have been no incidents of aggression/violence, he seems settled where he is. No conflict has arisen as of yet [about five months since admission]. As the young person is beginning to show remorse for past offences, the use of RJ would help/promote these feelings.'

In other cases, there was documented evidence that RJ had been used, but it was unclear whether it was having any impact:

'Evidence of use of RJ but not enough evidence to substantiate its effect. [Examples include] RJ meeting – assaulted staff and destroyed somebody else's property. Reparation – to clean up mess, do school work and apologise to people. Street RJ – refusal to settle at bedtime – no reparation, refused to accept responsibility.'

More positive comments include the following:

'... this young person responds well to RA (restorative approaches). He understands wrongdoing, is protective of staff, has anger management problems and has problems recognising this. He is motivated by incentive schemes. Likes to be part of familiar surroundings and with consistent adult carers who he will listen to when RA is being used.'

In some cases 'the loss of' or 'missing' things was seen as reparation (see Table 7.6). This was a practice also mentioned in a number of manager and staff group interviews (see Chapter Five).

It seemed clear in these cases that staff went through the process of encounter with a young person but did not follow through to reparation. Interviews with staff in Chapter Five illustrated that this related to confusion about the meaning of 'reparation' for some staff and a belief that an apology was somehow not enough. However, case files did show that in other cases there was evidence of an approach more in keeping with the RJ philosophy. Some examples follow in Table 7.7.

Impact of care

Staff were asked to rate the impact on young people of four aspects of living in residential care. The overall assessment of these 16 individuals presents a complex picture (see Table 7.8). Behaviour towards adults and other young people is at least 'OK' in the majority of cases, with a positive impact being seen in at least half the

Table 7.6: Case studies: examples of 'loss of' and 'missing' things as 'reparation'

Focus of RJ	Type of RJ	Reparation?
Abusive language	Informal	Pocket money frozen
Making rude noises despite being asked not to	Informal	Loss of settling-down time with staff member for one day
Disrespectful towards staff – rude and abusive. Threats of physical violence.	Informal	To miss one hour of TV
'Mispers'	Formal – impromptu conference	Loss of TV/computer
Targeting a female member of staff	Formal conference	To miss next planned trip out

Table 7.7: Case studies: examples of 'apology' and 'help' as reparation

Focus of RJ	Type of RJ	Reparation?
Verbal and physical abuse	Informal	Apologise for behaviour
Kept staff up late	Informal	Washing up – young person's suggestion
Young person victim of an assault	Informal	Apology from aggressor
Complaint by a young person – about a member of staff	Formal	Apology from member of staff

cases. On balance, the assessment of the impact on education is most positive and the impact on offending behaviour is most mixed (seen as 'very negative' in the case of four individuals). In these four cases, three individuals had a record of offending at the time of admission to care. Similarly, the individual with a very negative assessment in terms of their behaviour towards adults had a record of offending at the time of admission to care.

Conclusion

This chapter presents a complex picture of what happens to a group of children and young people in residential care over time. Offending behaviour is even more prevalent in our study than has been shown in previous studies (see, for example, Darker et al, 2008). There are a number of possible explanations for this. One is that children and young people in residential care in this local authority are more problematic than in other studies. Another relates to practice: either staff were worse at managing behaviour or the criminal justice system was more punitive (or 'effective'?) in relation to detecting offending behaviour in our local authority. There are also methodological reasons; for example, it is likely that in our study, cross-checking against agency records (those of social services and the YOT) uncovered

Table 7.8: Case studies: overall assessment of impact of care

	Very negative	Negative	OK	Positive	Very positive	No change
Behaviour towards adults (in the home)	1	1	5	7	2	
Behaviour towards other young people (in the home)	0	1	7	7	1	
Young people's education	0	2	2	5	5	2 *(not a problem at start of placement)*
Offending behaviour	4	1	2	1	4	2 *(not a problem at start of placement)* 2 *(of those in secure accommodation)*

N = 16, all of the case studies

more records of offending behaviour than would have been found through one source of information only. The level of access we had to case file data (via care staff) and the willingness of staff to follow up missing information on individuals was another factor in our study, as was the longitudinal nature of our research, where we followed through what happened over a year in the cohort study and several months in the case studies. We also had good access to evidence of what happened before an episode of care. In this way, we have avoided the pitfall of taking a snapshot of what is known about levels of offending at just one point in time and, possibly as a result of this, we have uncovered more evidence of offending.

The preceding chapters have presented various aspects of issues that relate to and affect young people's behaviour. It is clear from these chapters that aggressive behaviour is very common in the residential care environment, as is going missing and unauthorised absence. Together these problems are a volatile mix and one that enhances the risk of offending behaviour, either through peer influence (from other residents in the home) or through being away from adult control (when going missing or on unauthorised absence) and therefore more likely to be involved in survival crimes (such as theft).

Nevertheless, some aspects of care are judged to be positive for some young people. Of note is the association between positive educational experiences and young people who do not offend. This latter observation is supported by a great deal of wider research on the protective effects of schooling and education (Graham, 1988; Farrington, 1996; Hayden, 2007).

Evidence of any impact of RJ on the behaviour of individual young was limited, either because evidence was simply not recorded or, in cases where events and responses were recorded, because there no evaluation. In other cases, it was clear that RJ was used informally, as we have seen in earlier chapters, primarily as a style of communication, as the following quote illustrates:

> 'RAs [restorative approaches] are used frequently to resolve issues around the home to help this young person understand how his behaviour can impact on others. To also help him with better decision making etc, which he is working hard to improve on.'

From Wagga Wagga[1] to the children's home

8

Did restorative justice fulfil its promise?

Restorative justice (RJ) has some passionate advocates and, as we noted in Chapter One, its time has come in the wider policy context in Britain. Neither of the authors of this volume could be described as 'evangelical' or naive (Dignan, 2003, p 135) about the likely transformative impact of RJ in a context such as children's residential care (see also Daly, 2002); rather, we set out to take a careful and evidenced look at how it was implemented across 10 very different children's residential homes. Overall, the findings from our empirical research reinforce Daly's advice that we should expect modest and patchy results from the approach rather than the 'nirvana story' that is often communicated (Daly, 2002). We hope our investigation fulfils the need to move to a 'new' phase in our understanding of RJ that leaves behind the polar opposites of optimism without empirical evidence and scepticism when the new approach becomes familiar and the impossible dreams of change are not realised (Daly, 2002). A new phase for research into RJ has to be a move away from commentaries that focus on single case studies of extraordinary people who forgive, repent or change and move on from horrific or harmful behaviour.

Our research findings are rather more mixed than those in Littlechild's (2003) research. The manager of the children's home that was the focus of Littlechild's research describes the introduction of RJ in that home in the following way:

> 'Staff had decided not to tell the children about the introduction of RJ because they had anxieties about sharing their thoughts and feelings with them – they were worried the children would use this information against them. However, within a few months the young people, specifically the older ones, could be heard using the restorative questions to deal with disputes amongst themselves. There was less aggression, more cuddles, and the children said Stanfield was a "nicer place to live".... My only regret is that I didn't discover RJ thirty-seven years ago when my career in residential social work began!' (Hart, 2006, p 2)

There were certainly individual staff members who were equally enthusiastic about RJ in our research. There were also homes that were generally positive about RJ and its uses in the residential childcare setting. Inevitably, though, the picture varied across the 10 homes, partly because of staff attitudes and dynamics within homes and partly because the homes faced different challenges and circumstances that could get in the way of focusing on implementing the approach. Issues such as staffing, volatile new admissions, home refurbishments, relocation and so on could make it difficult for some homes and staff to focus on RJ.

In this chapter, we make a number of observations regarding our evidence about the impact of implementing an RJ approach in 10 children's homes and issues to be resolved in relation to the practicalities of using this approach in this type of environment. In doing so, we hope to make broader observations about the logistics of RJ policy transfer into children's residential care. As our study was informed by realist principles, it is not a matter of simply concluding that it either worked or did not work. It should also be noted that important parts of the data gathering depended on the efforts of staff within the local authority and police service. Their cooperation greatly improved the range and depth of data available in this study. The cohort study depended centrally on staff in children's services setting up a tracking system and helping the researchers to add data on education and offending. The case studies depended on residential staff collating data from case files, while police call-out data were collated by the local constabulary. The researchers in this study were thus afforded access to a wide variety of data and situations and this inevitably leads to a 'warts and all' picture of events. It is a brave organisation that allows this sort of access and it is something that was greatly respected and appreciated by the researchers.

We have already noted that the research was carried out in the context of constantly changing circumstances in the care homes studied. This is often the case in a real-world setting and our evaluative approach takes this into account. The closure of two homes in early 2007 and the temporary relocation of one of the remaining eight homes later in 2007 (due to refurbishment) were important considerations. Furthermore, the local authority had been bringing back young people from out-of-county placements since 2005, potentially increasing the challenges staff faced in terms of managing conflict. It is important to bear these issues in mind as we highlight our conclusions and make an overall judgement on the evidence collated.

Table 8.1 presents an overview of our conclusions from the different types of data gathered in the study. Table 8.2 reformulates these conclusions using a realist format. Overall, Table 8.1 shows that there was a positive shift in staff attitudes over a one-year period as they came to grips with implementing the RJ approach, although it should be noted that not all staff were persuaded of its benefits. Children often had an intuitive understanding of RJ, even if they did not understand the formal terms used. Institutional data on incident records, police call-outs and use of the out-of-hours service all showed a reduction following the implementation of RJ. Offending levels remained the same. Table 8.2 also highlights some of the issues or themes surrounding RJ in the residential care context; we go on to discuss these later in this chapter. Overall our study represents a positive (if patchy) set of outcomes from implementing an RJ approach, given the wider pressures on the service as well as attitudes towards these young people within the community. Our study points to a number of important issues about how restorative justice is conceptualised and used with children in a residential setting.

Table 8.1: Overview of conclusions from data collected in the research

Data types and sources	Conclusions
Care staff and managers (questionnaires and interviews)	*Positive shift in attitudes* towards the approach (statistically significant). Managers more positive than care staff. *RJ mostly used informally*, full conferences rare. External facilitators not available. *Divisions in some staff groups* more obvious during second visits. *Reparation* not a feature of around a third of encounters.
Children (questionnaires and interviews)	*Staff expectations* about behaviour – understood by the majority. *Staff accessibility and support* – most felt that staff would talk things through or help as needed. *Clarity of rules and staff fairness* – views were divided. *Understanding of RJ* – 42.1% knew what RJ meant, the remainder did not or were unsure; more showed an intuitive understanding when giving examples of how problems were, or should be, dealt with.
Context and process (observations during fieldwork and in meetings and presentations with staff)	*Big changes in evidence across the service* in a one-year period, including the closure of two homes and the investigation of another in relation to the use of physical interventions. There were also changes in residents (some more, some less volatile than their predecessors) and a change of management in one home. Despite *some loss of momentum* staff did have *refresher training* and *meetings continued* in relation to promoting the approach across the service.
Outcomes for children (cohort study and case studies)	*High levels of offending and incidents* in homes. *Importance of education* for those not in trouble. *Use and impact of RJ variable* at the individual level.
Organisational change: outcome indicators (organisational trend data on offending, police call-outs, incident records and out-of-hours service)	*No change in rate of offending,* but rate of offending increased in the general population. *Positive change in three sets of organisational records:* incident records; police call-outs; out-of-hours service.

Table 8.2: Realist conclusions to the research

Contexts (those features of the conditions in which programmes are introduced that are relevant to the operation of the programme mechanisms)
RJ was implemented in very different types of children's residential care homes; it was a useful tool in all types of home, but met with more success in homes with staff who saw the broader relevance of the approach. Care staff working with younger children did not always like/see the relevance of the focus on offending behaviour. Care staff in secure homes were more confident in the use of the approach and voluntarism was not seen as an option; children were expected to resolve conflict within an RJ encounter. The timing in the use of RJ was crucial in all settings; it had to be immediate enough (as people had to go on living and working together) but also timely in relation to the young person being calm enough and willing to talk things through.
Mechanisms (what it is about programmes or interventions that is likely to bring about an effect)
Most staff used informal RJ as a style or way of communicating or in impromptu conferences or 'encounters' to help resolve everyday conflicts within children's homes. This approach was viewed as a way of resolving conflict as well as a way of modelling wanted or pro-social behaviour.
Desired outcomes (what the adoption of an RJ approach is trying to achieve)
Some reduction in conflict but no reduction in official records of offending behaviour; some improvement in perceptions of residential homes as better places to live and work; evidence of staff/homes 'owning more of their conflicts' by fewer calls to the police, incident records and calls to the out-of-hours service. It appears that any learning in terms of managing conflict or behaving in a pro-social manner did not transfer to situations outside the home, partly because the response of people outside the home could not be controlled or predicted.

Conceptualising restorative justice

Whether RJ could fulfil its promise in our study depended, to a great extent, on what the organisation (the local authority), home managers and care staff expected of it. In our research, there were two clear alternative conceptualisations of RJ. These conceptualisations mirror what Gavrielides (2008) characterised as 'pragmatic' and 'abolitionist' understandings.

Pragmatic accounts

A number of staff considered RJ as another useful tool to use alongside more orthodox care work practice. The following quotes are indicative of the views of those staff who saw few transformative aspects to the care role within the restorative justice paradigm but stressed its complementary aspects. For these staff, the restorative processes of 'encounter' and 'communication' to solve conflict was something they had always done in their professional role.

'RJ is a bit of a joke in that it was like teaching granny to suck eggs for most of the time ... it's just common sense.'

'RJ is existing practice given a politically correct name.'

'We were already doing it before training, not knowing it was RJ … [it is] just slightly different questions.'

As a direct result of this pragmatic conceptualisation, specific aspects of RJ were incorporated by some care homes to bolster existing practice rather than seek to fundamentally alter it. One example in the secure children's home in this study is where an emphasis on the encounter between offender and victim enabled the home to incorporate meetings between young people in conflict into their methods of dealing with such conflict. This was done with an emphasis on the *absence* of choice or empowerment.

'We do a lot of restorative justice because we've got a captive audience. So if there is an incident or conflict between young people they're not going anywhere. They are not able to run away. They're not able to avoid it [the RJ approach], so at whatever point we think it is correct to do it we can get young people together … we just cannot have two kids at loggerheads. Whereas in an open unit one young person can run off.'

Staff in the secure children's home were introduced to the 'encounter' concept in their training and saw it as a useful way of ensuring order and control in the environment, as the young people were expected to sit and communicate with each other during such encounters. This involved a certain amount of change in that staff said they had previously tended to talk to young people individually about interpersonal conflict rather than bring the main protagonists together to resolve the issue. On reflection, they realised that they were expecting young people to resolve things between themselves, without mediation or adult help. Within the secure home environment, care staff valued the RJ approach, as it was compatible with the running and institutional agenda of the home. It gave staff a way of dealing with conflicts that ensured no lasting resentment or anger, which was seen as the key to maintaining a calm atmosphere. Staff in the secure environment did not incorporate the notion of 'voluntarism' into their practice, as this would have given the young people the power to make their own decisions about whether or not to resolve a conflict. Such devolution of power to the children would have challenged existing care practice in a highly controlled environment such as this. Allowing the main protagonists a certain amount of power would have resulted in conflicts within the secure home being left unresolved or continuing for longer than necessary.

The approach to RJ encounters in the secure home contrasted sharply with that in the open homes. Here, the relative 'freedoms' the young people enjoyed could result in them walking out of the home with staff being largely powerless to stop them. Staff therefore remoulded the restorative approaches they had learned during their training, leading to very fluid conceptualisations that did not have the formality of an encounter and often involved discussions solely with the offender or ad hoc solutions applied as soon as the incident or harmful behaviour had taken place. As we have already documented, formalised restorative conferences or mediation sessions requiring planning, scripts or prescribed roles were deemed to be largely impractical and often inappropriate in the care environment. Such formalised encounters were either considered to take too long to arrange or were perceived by the young people to resemble formalised criminal justice systems where care staff could be seen as 'judge and jury'. As a result, staff in open homes tended to have a more fluid approach to RJ that took notions of 'voluntarism' seriously.

However, the absence of more formalised restorative approaches in the open homes sometimes led to a failure to record the restorative encounter or to take the necessary steps to ensure that reparation to the victim took place. 'Stand-up' restorative justice was used very quickly after the event and there was less attention to constructing written plans to resolve the situation or initiating formal agreements between young people. While this is an important aspect of restorative approaches, it was not a priority, as it simply did not fit into the reality of running a busy children's home.

There was a strong view among care home staff in the study that restorative justice was either existing childcare practice given a new name or an identifiable set of practices that staff could keep in their 'professional toolbox' and use when the circumstances were deemed appropriate. In some cases, restorative justice practices were blended to complement existing approaches, with the challenging aspects of the paradigm ignored in order to maintain the status quo in terms of professional knowledge, values and practice.

Abolitionist accounts

Another conceptualisation of restorative justice evident in the research was more challenging of the existing professional care role. Here, RJ was seen as an alternative paradigm of care that had inherent tensions with traditional approaches (Gavrielides, 2008). Restorative justice values were often discussed as *changing practice* and offering *challenges* to staff. Significantly, RJ challenged the existing power relations between staff and children in the homes, giving some power to the protagonists in conflict to communicate and attempt to agree a resolution to their dispute. This could mean that staff did not dictate the outcomes and ways in which to make the amends necessary to move the situation on. Some comments from staff demonstrated more abolitionist conceptualisations that challenged their existing professional care work, close to what Olson and Dzur (2004, p 145) called restorative justice as 'a programme of professional renewal'. For these staff, restorative justice meant changes to existing practice and power relations, and new challenges, as the following quotes illustrate:

'The biggest turnaround in work practice I've ever seen.'

'RJ approaches may mean that staff feel a loss of control, a loss of face but this is the challenge to care practice.'

'We have a lot of debates in staff meetings…. We have a therapeutic approach to our work…. We ask ourselves, "Are we moulding to fit RJ?", "Is it alright if we move RJ towards us?"…. Because it's so new it's just raising questions.'

Where care staff appreciated the role RJ could have in underpinning cultural change, they were able to document examples of where RJ had had a transformative impact. In one home that recorded high satisfaction rates with restorative approaches, staff said the home had been transformed from being a place where there was an atmosphere of conflict between staff and young people to one where there was a sense of shared ownership in making the home a peaceful and productive environment. This home had largely ended the practice of fines or sanctions as punishment and had agreed a range of outcomes designed to make amends to the victims of harmful behaviour. One member of staff encapsulated the change in staff and young people's relationships by describing how restorative approaches had resulted in a change in the culture of the home from "'them and us' … to 'all'".

Nevertheless, the abolitionist conceptualisation involving professional and personal change was not the dominant one expressed by staff interviewed for the research. Some were more willing than others to adapt their practice to restorative processes such as meetings, communications and encounters between themselves and young people. Some homes had made less headway into challenging and replacing the culture of fines, sanctions and removal of services as a response to problem behaviour. In addition, the loss of power and authority inherent in some of RJ values remained an unresolved issue for certain members of staff.

Restorative justice in the children's residential care environment

Just as our research highlights the dangers of uncritically transferring well-established restorative processes from other environments into residential care without consideration of the peculiarities of the care environment, so it is important to discuss the impact the implementation of restorative justice had on care staff roles. As Olson and Dzur (2004) have noted, RJ theory has largely ignored the role of professionals in the criminal justice process and yet professionals are crucially important if RJ is to be implemented successfully.

The initial training for staff communicated the idea that the RJ 'gold standard' was the formal, scripted, restorative conference with the established roles of *victim, offender* and trained *mediator* (see Figure 8.1 below, and Raye and Roberts, 2007, p 228). As we have already discussed, care staff soon realised that such formal scripted approaches would have a limited impact on the care environment and would possibly make relationships between young people and staff more problematic. More fluid restorative processes would have to be developed and this resulted in what has been called 'stand-up' or 'corridor' RJ in work with schools (see, for example, Morrison, 2001). By the second period of field research, most staff referred to restorative *approaches*, rather than restorative justice, because they wanted to emphasise the difference between their approach and that of the youth justice system. Furthermore, much of the behaviour tackled through restorative approaches was not necessarily criminal.

McCluskey and colleagues (2008) have alerted us to some of the problems of transposing the criminal justice terminology and roles specified in most conceptualisations of RJ to the school environment. They also highlight how this can be problematic for children with complex lives and emotions. Indeed, the prescribed roles of victim, offender and mediator were hugely problematic in the residential care environment for children and staff alike. The notion that children in care should occupy offender/perpetrator or victim roles in an RJ encounter left many staff feeling uncomfortable. They felt they were ascribing blame to a particular child when all of the children could be seen as victims, at least in the sense that they had been removed from their families and were being looked after in a children's home, and perhaps also because of what had happened to them before they came into care. Furthermore, the fluid nature of interpersonal relationships in residential care meant it was difficult to ascribe static roles. One member of staff summed up the position well in their comments on the criminal justice system:

> '[Often] people don't know each other, [therefore] the "victim" and "offender" is clear. Here [in residential care] people know each other, it's not the same. It's not always clear who is the victim and who is the offender. There's history.'

However, while it was necessary to adapt the restorative approach to make it more appropriate for use in a residential childcare setting, problems arose in maintaining its central philosophy. More broadly, transposing a generic model of restorative justice unearthed issues of accountability and fairness. In our research, the prescribed roles that are usually attributed to restorative approaches were not felt to be applicable and residential care staff themselves would facilitate whichever restorative approach they considered appropriate, such as an encounter between two young people in conflict, rather than employ an independent external mediator. This required staff to occupy roles that were in some ways familiar to the traditional restorative facilitator or mediator role (as in Figure 8.1) but notably different in other ways (Schiff, 2007, p 228). In our study, residential care staff would ensure that all young people had their say and were allowed to express their feelings and wishes in a non-confrontational way, akin to Braithwaite's ideal of non-domination (Braithwaite, 2003, cited in Johnstone and Van Ness, 2007a). However, care staff also had organisational pressures to contend with, centring on safety for all children within the home. We have indicated above how this compromised the ideal of voluntarism in the secure home.

Figure 8.1: Roles in the 'victim–offender mediation' model of restorative justice

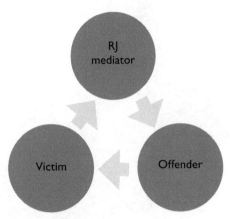

Source: Based on Raye and Warner Roberts, 2007, p 219

The clarity of roles was further complicated by the fact that care staff would often find themselves in the situation of being victimised by a young person and required to undertake a restorative meeting with that same young person in their role as a member of staff trained in restorative approaches. This is arguably more problematic when adult professionals are victimised by powerless young people (even though young people may not be perceived as powerless). There are two reasons for this. First, a central concept of the restorative justice paradigm is the centrality of the victim's wishes and second, power relations are significant when making amends for the harm caused.

Where staff are the victims of harmful behaviour by young people, it is not so easy for them to adopt the role of victim in the restorative process. Staff may be reluctant to share their feelings of being victimised by the young person for fear of 'losing face' or power over the situation, and they may feel that an expression of vulnerability will be used by the young person to victimise them again at a later stage. The fact that the victimised member of staff on a particular shift in the home would sometimes also be responsible for ensuring that a restorative event occurred further compounded the problematic nature of power relations in the home. Indeed, it could be argued that in these circumstances the roles of 'victim', 'mediator' (or 'facilitator') and 'staff member' are unworkable and highly problematic in ensuring the successful implementation of restorative approaches. Figure 8.2 demonstrates that in responding to harmful events and conflict within the home, the roles of staff could involve a complex interplay of 'victim' (feeling victimised), 'facilitator' (ensuring that the role was dealt with by a restorative approach) and 'residential staff member or state functionary' (ensuring that the harmful event did not affect the security of other residents in the home). As such, the roles within common conceptualisations of restorative justice were very fluid in the children's home, involving obvious power imbalances that were highly problematic.

Figure 8.2: Interplay of care staff roles in a restorative justice encounter

The fluidity of staff roles had major implications for staff members who had been assaulted and wanted to call the police to question the young person involved, but, in their capacity as restorative facilitators, also felt under pressure to deal with the situation without recourse to criminal justice agencies. Staff emphasised how sensitive the issue of 'making amends' could be when the victim was an adult member of staff and as such remained in a powerful position. For example, in one incident a member of staff had been the victim of harmful behaviour and had received an 'apology' by the young person involved. The young person built on her apology, making amends by cooking the member of staff a breakfast. While this was appreciated by the member of staff in question, she commented in the research that she could never have suggested this course of action herself, because she would have felt as if she were abusing her power as a care professional. Furthermore, the power relations inherent in working with children were discussed when staff were asked to consider whether apologising and making amends was appropriate when the professional could also be seen to be responsible for conflict in the home. This was seen as a further challenge to the traditional care staff role and the desire of some staff to have power and authority at all times (McLeod, 2007). Such tension within roles, particularly where staff had been victimised, was also related to the unhappiness of some staff who saw RJ as part of a management agenda to reduce the number of calls to the police.

While these are highly specific instances, they serve once again to reflect the difficulties in successfully transferring restorative processes, roles and values from one environment to another without a full exploration of the logistics involved. In our research, the development of restorative outcomes remained embryonic, which was to be expected in view of the sensitivity and power relations inherent when adult professionals are victimised by young people in a model that prioritises the victim's wishes and demands for reparation.

In interpreting the positive results from trends in most of the organisational data (incident records, calls to the police and out-of-hours service), it is useful to refer to the work of Christie (1977). The decrease in the number of staff appeals for external help in response to incidents in the homes reflects a central value of the restorative justice paradigm, in that successful informal justice means that communities deal with problems themselves, with the main protagonists being central to the process and the victim's wishes and demands being particularly important (Christie, 1977). Here children's homes can be seen as moving towards 'owing their own conflicts', both in terms of the internal processes used to deal with problem behaviour and the outcomes and consequences to the harm caused. In one of the homes in the study, a manager informed the researchers that the restorative justice model had given her relatively inexperienced staff a language and value system with which to engage with children in a communicative way that was previously missing. Significant numbers of staff indicated that young people in the home had benefited from being allowed to communicate their feelings of anger or hurt and to deal with conflicts in a positive and non-confrontational manner. The reduction in the number of incident reports and use of the out-of-hours service bears witness to a decrease in the number of significant incidents reported by the home, after a period of time during which such incidents had been increasing. However, staff did feel that progress was slow and patchy, with some children seemingly immune to the effect of the restorative approach. Staff often discussed a lack of investment and ownership in the children's home by some children (indicated by the high level of children going missing) and the ineffectiveness of the approach where there was a limited sense of 'community and belonging':

> 'Until the kids have a relationship with the staff and an investment in living in the unit, we have nothing to use in an RJ approach.'

More broadly, staff also saw positive benefits to young people in using restorative approaches:

> 'It teaches them good conflict resolution skills ... their grudges do build up and they gang up on each other.... It does teach them how to get along with people, even if they don't like them.'

> 'It's helped the children take more responsibility, definitely, definitely.'

Children often showed an intuitive understanding of RJ or restorative approaches, with some able to articulate important aspects of the value base. This was most evident in the way they wanted or saw problems or conflicts resolved, as the concept was not always easily understood. Many indicated an understanding of restorative concepts and were willing to do something positive rather than receive a sanction for problem behaviour.

While there is evidence in our research of a reduction in the number of serious incidents occurring within the home, and some evidence of an improvement in relationships between staff and young people, there remains an important caveat to this relatively successful implementation of RJ in residential childcare. Our data demonstrate that the criminalisation rate for looked after children did not decrease during the period of implementation of restorative justice. Official records of offending remained high (11.2% rate for all children in local authority care and much higher for those in residential care) after the implementation of an RJ approach. The involvement of restorative justice approaches in broader terms across agencies within the local authority remained unresolved. Where young people in residential care committed offences or harmful behaviour in the community (that is, outside of the home), there were limited attempts to operationalise a restorative justice response and few successes. Indeed, one could argue that restorative justice often began and ended at the front door of the home. There were attempts at involving neighbours where their property had been damaged and some were successful. However, there was sometimes a reluctance on the part of members of the wider community to meet the young people and take part in a restorative approach. Furthermore, our research found that other criminal justice agencies, notably the police, were unreliable restorative partners, reacting unpredictably to the protocol to participate in the restorative approaches with children in care.

In addition, the local authority was operating in a somewhat hostile climate towards youth crime and residential children's homes. A number of homes had problematic relationships with neighbours; in one case, local residents, with the support of their Member of Parliament, were campaigning to have a home closed down. Many local shops had policies that indicated they would *always* prosecute young offenders rather than participate in any restorative approach. Moreover, in order for a home to achieve successful implementation of restorative justice and diversion from the criminal justice system, it would have to raise its profile and encourage interaction between young people and the local community. This was counter to the prevailing trend in a number of homes to actively seek to *minimise* their presence in the local community in order to ensure the home's future existence. As a result, in cases where young people offended outside the residential home environment, there was limited use of restorative approaches and outcomes. Little progress had been made in our research into harnessing the power of the local community to address problem behaviour by children in care or providing services and links between homes and local communities to develop fully a sense of social inclusion and belonging (White, 2003). There existed a policy gap between restorative approaches to problem behaviour inside and outside the home. As a result, children in care continued to be overrepresented in the ranks of those entering the criminal justice system.

We conclude with a reflection on why, despite some of the problematic aspects, we believe implementing restorative approaches within children's residential care is worthwhile. We recognise that cultural change within organisations and institutions takes time. McClusky and colleagues (2008) suggest that it may take between five and 10 years to embed major change in the values and practices of schools. Our case study local authority had already begun to introduce the values underpinning a restorative approach to harm and wrongdoing through its adoption of the Team-Teach (2003) approach to managing behaviour and avoiding the need for physical restraint (see Chapter Three). These changes are very much in keeping with the evolving practice and value base in residential care, as well as evidence about 'what works' best in these settings. They also accord well with the intentions of contemporary policy (Hopkins, 2008). Encounter and communication are crucial to resolving interpersonal conflict; they are also important in the development of social skills and understanding, as well as the modelling of pro-social behaviour. Finally, restorative approaches must surely be a better way of resolving conflict with vulnerable children who have lost and missed out on so much than the punitive approaches still apparent in the 'loss of' and 'missing' opportunities responses to some problem behaviour (see Chapter Seven).

Note:
[1] Wagga Wagga has an important place in the history and development of restorative justice and has attracted significant academic attention. It is usually referred to as the area of Australia that first trialled the family group conference model. The 'Wagga model', as it became known, was an approach whereby a facilitator would read a script in order to facilitate the meeting and all parties in the dispute would remain in the room throughout the decision-making process (see Sherman, 2001, p 35; Raye and Roberts, 2007, p 211).

References

Aries, P. (1960) *Centuries of Childhood*, Harmondsworth: Penguin.

Axford, N. (2010) Is social exclusion a useful concept in children's services?, *British Journal of Social Work*, vol 40, no 3, pp 737-54.

Barnardo's (2006) Barnardo's Statement of Ethical Research Practice, www.barnardos. org.uk/ethical.pdf

Bazemore, G. (1998) Restorative justice and earned redemption, *American Behavioural Scientist*, vol 41, no 6, pp 768-813.

Berridge, D. (2007) Theory and explanation in child welfare: education and looked-after children, *Child and Family Social Work*, 12, pp 1-10.

Berridge, D. and Brodie, I. (1998) *Children's Homes Revisited*, London: Jessica Kingsley Publishers.

Biehal, N., Clayden, J., Stein, M. and Wade, J. (1995) *Moving On*, HMSO: London.

Braithwaite, J. (1989) *Crime, Shame and Reintegration*, Cambridge: Cambridge University Press.

Braithwaite, J. and Parker, C. (1999) Restorative justice is republican justice, in S. Walgrave and S.G. Bazemore (eds) *Restorative Juvenile Justice: Repairing the Harm of Youth Crime*, International Network for Research on Restorative Justice for Juveniles, Monsey, NY: Criminal Justice Press.

Broad, B. (2005) Young people leaving care: implementing the Children (Leaving Care) Act 2000?, *Children & Society*, vol 19, no 5, pp 371-84.

Cameron, R.J. and Maginn, C. (2009) *Achieving Positive Outcomes for Children in Care*, Sage Publications: London.

Campbell, V. (2009) Editorial: a prejudice that needs to be shifted, *Children Webmag*, 1 July, www.childrenwebmag.com

Christie, N. (1977) Conflicts as property, *British Journal of Criminology*, vol 17, no 1, pp 1-15.

Cliffe, D. with Berridge, D. (1991) *Closing Children's Homes. An End to Residential Childcare?*, London: National Children's Bureau.

Clough, R., Bullock, R. and Ward, A. (2006) *What Works in Residential Child Care: A Review of Research Evidence and the Practical Considerations*, London: National Children's Bureau.

Coldrey, B. (2001) 'The extreme end of a spectrum of violence': physical abuse, hegemony and resistance in British residential child care, *Children & Society*, vol 15, no 2, pp 95-106.

CPS (Crown Prosecution Service) (2006) Guidance on the prosecution of offending behaviour in children's homes, www.cps.gov.uk

Crawford, A. and Newburn, T. (2003) *Youth Offending and Restorative Justice. Implementing Reform in Youth Justice*, Cullompton: Willan Publishing.

Daly, K. (2002) Restorative justice. The real story, *Punishment & Society*, vol 4, no 1, pp 55-79.

Daly, K. and Immarigeon, R. (1998) The past, present and future of restorative justice, *Contemporary Justice Review*, vol 1, no 1, pp 21-47.

Darker, I., Ward, H. and Caulfield, L. (2008) An analysis of offending by young people looked after by local authorities, *Youth Justice*, vol 8, no 2, pp 134-48.

DCSF (Department for Children, Schools and Families) (2002) *Choice protects*, London: DCSF.

DCSF (2003) *Every child matters*, London: DCSF.

DCSF (2005) Children's workforce strategy consultation document, www.ttrb.ac.uk/viewarticle2.aspx?contentId=10867

DCSF (2006) *Care matters: Transforming the lives of children and young people in care*, London: DCSF.

DCSF (2009a) *Outcome Indicators for Children Looked After: Twelve Months to 30 September 2008, England*, SFR 07/2009, 30 April, London: DCSF, www.dcsf.gov.uk/rsgateway/DB/SFR/s000842/SFR07_2009PDF_Ammended_251109.pdf

DCSF (2009b) *Children Looked After in England (Including Adoption and Care Leavers) Year Ending 31 March 2009*, SFR 25/2009, 13 October, London: DCSF, www.dcsf.gov.uk/rsgateway/DB/SFR/s000878/SFR25-2009Version2.pdf

DCSF (2009c) *Children Leaving Care – Every Child Matters*, London: DCSF, www.dcsf.gov.uk/everychildmatters/safeguardingandsocialcare/childrenleavingcare

DCSF (2009e) *Targeted Youth Support (TYS)*, London: DCSF, www.dcsf.gov.uk/everychildmatters/Youth/youthmatters/connexions/targetedyouthsupport/tys

DfES (Department for Education and Skills) (2003) *Every Child Matters*, London: DFES.

DfES (2007) *Care Matters*, London: DFES.

DH (Department of Health) (1998) *Quality Protects: Framework for Action*, London: DH.

DH (1999) *Me Survive Out There? New Arrangements for Young People Living in and Leaving Care*, London: DH.

DH (2002) *Promoting the Health of Looked After Children*, London: DH.

Dignan, J. (2003) Towards a systemic model of restorative justice: reflections on the concept, its context and the need for clear restraints, in A. Von Hirsch, J. Roberts, A.E. Bottoms, K. Roach and M. Schiff (eds) *Restorative Justice and Criminal Justice: Competing or Reconcilable Paradigms?*, Oxford: Hart Publications.

Farrington, D. (1996) *Understanding and Preventing Youth Crime*, York: York Publishing Services Ltd/Joseph Rowntree Foundation.

Farrington, D.P. (2002) Key findings from the first 40 years of the Cambridge Study in Delinquent Development, in T.P. Thornbury and M.D. Krohn (eds) *Taking Stock of Delinquency: An Overview of Findings from Contemporary Longitudinal Studies*, New York, NY: Luwer/Plenum.

Frost, N. and Stein, M. (1989) *The Politics of Child Welfare: Inequality, Power and Change*, London: Harvester Wheatsheaf.

Garland, D. (2001) *The Culture of Control*, Oxford: Oxford University Press.

Gavrielides, T. (2008) Restorative justice – the perplexing concept: conceptual fault lines and power battles within the restorative justice movement, *Criminology and Criminal Justice*, vol 8, no 2, pp 165-83.

Goldson, B. (2000) Whither diversion? Interventionism and the new youth justice, in J. Pitts (ed) *The New Youth Justice*, Lyme Regis: Russell House Publishing.

Gorin, S. (2000) Managing to foster? Families' experience of caring for children away from home, Unpublished PhD thesis, University of Portsmouth.

Graham, J. (1988) *Schools, disruptive behaviour and delinquency: A review of research*, Home Office Research Study No 96, London: HMSO.

Gupta, A. and Blewett, J. (2007) Change for children? The challenges and opportunities for the children's social work workforce, *Child and Family Social Work*, vol 12, no 2, pp 172-81.

Haines, K. and O'Mahony, D. (2006) Restorative approaches, young people and youth justice, in B. Goldson and J. Muncie (eds) *Youth Crime and Justice: Critical Issues*, London: Sage Publications.

Harker, R. (2002) *Including Children in Social Research*, NCB Highlight No 193, London: National Children's Bureau.

Hart, V. (2006) Just care: RJ at Stanfield Home, Resolution, 21, News from the Restorative Justice Consortium, pp 2-3, www.restorativejustice.org.uk/Resources/pdf/n_letter_Winter_2006.pdf

Hayden, C. (1998) The use of physical restraint in children's residential care, *Social Services Research*, 3, pp 36-46.

Hayden, C. (2007) *Children in Trouble*, Basingstoke: Palgrave Macmillan.

Hayden, C. (2009) 'Family group conferences – are they an effective and viable way of working with attendance and behaviour problems in schools?', *British Journal of Educational Research*, vol 35, no 2, pp 205-20.

Hayden, C. and Gorin, S. (1998) 'Care and control of "Looked After" children in England', *International Journal of Child and Family Welfare*, no 3, pp 242-58.

Hayden, C., Goddard, J., Gorin, S. and Van Der Spek, N. (1999) *State Child Care. Looking After Children?*, London: Jessica Kingsley Publishers.

Hazel, N., Hagell, A., Liddle, M., Archer, D., Grimshaw, R. and King, J. (2002) *Detention and Training: Assessment of the Detention and Training Order and its Impact on the Secure Estate across England and Wales*, London: Youth Justice Board.

Hendrick, H. (1994) *Child Welfare: England 1872-1989*, London: Routledge.

Heptinstall, E. (2000) Gaining access to looked after children for research purposes: lessons learned, *British Journal of Social Work*, vol 30, no 6, pp 867-72.

Hills, J., Sefton, T. and Stewart, K. (eds) (2009) *Towards a More Equal Society? Poverty, inequality and policy since 1997*, Bristol: The Policy Press.

Home Office (1968) *Children in Trouble*. Cmnd 3601, London: HMSO.

Home Office (2004) *Preventative Approaches Targeting Young People in Local Authority Care*, Home Office Development and Practice Report 14, London: Home Office.

Hopkins, B. (2008) *Restorative Approaches in Residential Child Care*, NCB Highlight 242, Paper for the National Centre for Excellence in Residential Child Care. London: National Children's Bureau, www.ncb.org.uk/ncercc/ncercc%20practice%20documents/ncercc_restjustice_tcpaper.pdf

Home Office (2009) *Youth Crime Action Plan. One Year On*, London: Home Office.

Jackson, S. (1989) Residential care and education, *Children & Society*, vol 2, no 4, pp 335-50.

Johnstone, G. and Van Ness, D.W. (2007) The meaning of restorative justice, in G. Johnstone and D.W. Van Ness (eds) *Handbook of Restorative Justice*, Cullompton: Willan Publishing.

Kirkwood, A. (1993) *The Leicestershire Inquiry 1992*, Leicester: Leicestershire County Council.

Latimer, J., Dowden, C. and Muise, D. (2001) *The Effectiveness of Restorative Justice Practices: A Meta-Analysis*, Ottawa: Department of Justice Canada, Research and Statistics Division.

Little, M. (2000) The home guard, *Community Care*, 13 April, www.communitycare.co.uk/Articles/2000/04/13/7191/Th-home-guard.htm

Littlechild, B. (2003) *An Evaluation of the Implementation of a Restorative Justice Approach in a Residential Unit for Young People in Hertfordshire: Final Report*, Hatfield: University of Herfordshire.

MacDonald, R. and Marsh, J. (2001) Disconnected youth?, *Journal of Youth Studies*, vol 4, no 4, pp 373-91.

Marshall, T. (1999) *Restorative Justice. An Overview*, London: Home Office.

Marsh, K. (2008) To what extent are different types of care environment criminogenic?, MSc Thesis, *Internet Journal of Criminology*, www.internetjournalofcriminology.com/ijcundergrad.html

McClusky, G., Lloyd, G., Stead, J., Kane, J., Riddel, S. and Weedon, E. (2008) 'I was dead restorative today': from restorative justice to restorative approaches in school, *Cambridge Journal of Education*, vol 38, no 2, pp 199-216.

McLeod, A. (2007) Whose agenda? Issues of power and relationship when listening to looked-after children, *Child and Family Social Work*, vol 12, no 3, pp 278-86.

Millham, S., Bullock, R. and Cherret, P. (1975) *After Grace, Teeth*, London: Chaucer Publishing Company Ltd.

MORI (2005) *MORI Five-Year Report: An Analysis of Youth Survey Data*, London: Youth Justice Board.

Morrison, B. (2001) Developing the school's capacity in the regulation of civil society, in H. Strang and J. Braithwaite (eds) *Restorative Justice and Civil Society*, Cambridge: Cambridge University Press.

Muncie, J. and Goldson, B. (2006) England and Wales. The new correctionalism, in J. Muncie and B. Goldson (eds) *Comparative Youth Justice*, London: Sage Publications.

Nacro (2003) *Reducing Offending by Looked After Children. A Good Practice Handbook*, London: Nacro.

NCB (National Children's Bureau) (2007) *Care Matters: Time for Change*, NCB Member Briefing, London: NCB.

Olson, S.M. and Dzur, A.W. (2004) Revisiting informal justice: restorative justice and democratic professionalism, *Law and Society Review*, vol 38, no 1, pp 139-76.

O'Malley, P. (1999) Volatile and contradictory punishment, *Theoretical Criminology*, vol 3, no 2, pp 175-16.

Pawson, R. and Tilley, N. (2004) Realist evaluation, www.communitymatters.com. au/RE.

Polsky, H. (1962) *Cottage Six*, New York, NY: Russell Sage Foundation.

Raye, B.E. and Warner Roberts, A. (2007) Restorative processes, in G. Johnstone and D.W. Van Ness (eds) *The Handbook of Restorative Justice*, Cullompton: Willan Publishing.

Ritchie, C. (2005) Looked after children: time for change, *British Journal of Social Work*, vol 35, no 5, pp 761-7.

Robinson, G. and Shapland, J. (2008) Reducing recidivism: a task for restorative justice, *British Journal of Criminology*, vol 48, no 3, pp 337-59.

Roche, D. (2007) 'Retribution and restorative justice', in G. Johnstone and D. Van Ness (ed) *Handbook of Restorative Justice*, Willan: Cullompton, pp 75-90.

Rowlands, J. and Statham, J. (2009) Numbers of children looked after in England: a historical analysis, *Child & Family Social Work*, vol 14, no 1, pp 79-89.

Schiff, M. (2007) Satisfying the needs and interests of stakeholders, in G. Johnstone and D.W. Van Ness (eds) *Handbook of Restorative Justice*, Cullompton: Willan Publishing.

Sellick, C. (1998) The use of institutional care for children across Europe, *European Journal of Social Work*, vol 1, no 3, pp 301-10.

Sherman, L. (2001) 'Two Protestant ethics and the spirit of restoration', in H. Strang and J. Braithwaite (eds) *Restorative justice and civil society*, Cambridge: Cambridge University Press.

Sherman, L.W. and Strang, H. (2007) *Restorative Justice: The Evidence*, London: The Smith Institute.

Sinclair, I. and Gibb, I. (1998) *Children's Homes: A Study in Diversity*, Chichester: Wiley.

Smith, C. (1998) Incredible hulks: ship schools and the reformatory movement, *Emotional and Behavioural Difficulties*, vol 3, no 10, pp 20-4.

Stein, M. (2006b) Missing years of abuse in children's homes, *Child and Family Social Work*, vol 11, no 1, pp 11-21.

Stein, M. and Carey, K. (1986) *Leaving Care*, Oxford: Blackwell.

Strang, H. and Braithwaite, J. (eds) (2001) *Restorative Justice and Civil Society*, Cambridge: Cambridge University Press.

Taylor, C. (2003) Justice for looked after children?, *Probation Journal*, vol 50, no 3, pp 239-51.

Team-Teach (2003) *Team-Teach Workbook*, St. Leonards-on-Sea: Steaming Publications.

Tilley, N. (2009) *Crime Prevention*, Cullompton: Willan Publishing.

Törrönen, M. (2006) Community in a children's home, *Child and Family Social Work*, vol 11, no 2, pp 129-37.

Utting, Sir William (1997) *Review of the Safeguards for Children Living Away from Home*, London: DH/Welsh Office.

Van Ness, D.W. (2002) The shape of things to come: a framework for thinking about a restorative justice system, in E.G.M. Weitekamp and H.J. Kerner (eds) *Restorative Justice. Theoretical Foundations*, Cullompton: Willan Publishing.

Wachtel, T. (1999) Restoring community in a disconnected world, www.iirp.org/article_detail.php?article_id=NTEw

Wachtel, T. and McCold, P. (2001) Restorative justice in everyday life, in H. Strang and J. Braithwaite (eds) (2001) *Restorative Justice and Civil Society*, Cambridge: Cambridge University Press.

Waterhouse, R., Clough, M. and Le Fleming, M. (2000) *Lost in Care: Report of the Tribunal Enquiry into Abuse of Children in Care in the Former County Council Areas of Gwynedd and Clwyd Since 1974*, London: The Stationery Office.

White, K.J. (2008) Children and foster care: inclusion, exclusion and life chances, *Children Webmag*, 1 October, www.childrenwebmag.com/articles

White, R (2003) Communities, conferences and restorative social justice, *Criminal Justice*, vol 3 no 2, pp 139-60.

Willmott, N. (2007) *A Review of the Use of Restorative Justice in Children's Residential Care*, London: National Children's Bureau.

Wilson, D., Sharp, C. and Patterson, A. (2006) *Young People and Crime: Findings from the 2005 Offending, Crime and Justice Survey*, London: Home Office.

Wyler, S. (2000) *The Health of Young People Leaving Care*, London: The Kings Fund.

YJB (Youth Justice Board) (2001) *Risk and Protective Factors Associated with Youth Crime and Effective Interventions to Prevent It*, London: YJB.

YJB (2009) *Asset: Young Offenders Assessment Profile, Appendix B*, London: YJB, www. yjb.gov.uk/en-gb/practitioners/assessment/asset.htm

Young, J. (2002) Crime and social exclusion, in M. Maguire, R. Morgan and R. Reiner (eds) *The Oxford Handbook of Criminology* (3rd edn), Oxford: Oxford University Press, pp 457-90.

Zehr, H. (1990) *Changing Lens: A New Focus for Crime and Justice*, Scottdale: Herald Press.